UNCOVERING AND EMBRACING SOUL POWER

BEST PRACTICES FOR LEARNING THE ART OF SELF LOVE

EDWARD MILLER

Founder of SoulTranSync®

A SoulTranSync® Publication 2020

Publisher's Notes

Uncovering and Embracing Soul Power copyright 2020. Edward W. Miller, Author; SoulTranSync® Publishers.

This publication is designed to provide accurate and authoritative information in regards to the subject matter covered. It is sold with the understanding that the publisher is not engaged in rendering psychological, financial, legal or other professional services. If expert assistance or counting it is needed, the service of a competent professional should be sought.

No part of this publication may be reproduced, stored in a retrieval system or transmitted in any form or by any means except as permitted under Sections 107 or 108 of the 1976 U.S. Copyright Act, without written permission of the author/publisher or authorization through payment of the appropriate per-copy fee.

Requests for permission should be addressed to Edward W. Miller at SoulTranSync®, 1881 N.E. 26th Street Wilton Manors, FL 33305; soultransync@gmail.com; 866-714-7117.

ISBN 9780578675992/ 9780578675985

DEDICATION

I want to thank Jocelyn, my wife and soul partner for her unwavering devotion and loving commitment to me and my two daughters. I am so blessed to share my life, my love and all my passions with this beautiful and brilliant woman.

Table of Contents

PREFACE

In 2015, over several months, I experienced a crisis of faith and felt a pressing need for a break from facilitating my weekly Monday meditation group. I had been conducting this devotional self-awareness/ meditation group for over three years and my inspiration was beginning to wane. I had been professing that an end to suffering was possible, implying that I, myself, was free of suffering, but in fact, I was still deeply in pain.

For years I hadn't been able to sleep well most nights, staying awake worrying about every aspect of my life and unable to quiet my tormented mind. I was feeling inauthentic and frustrated with my progress as a teacher of spiritual awakening. I was also terrified that others would see that I was an imposter, illegitimately teaching concepts I wasn't capable of embracing myself. Even though I had been successful in inspiring others to awaken to their wholeness, my own story of inadequacy still haunted me when I lay down every night.

I realize now that I was still evolving in my own spiritual awareness and uncovering newer layers of unconscious resistance to the truth of my wholeness at the time. This spiritual crisis later became my motivation to awaken from the illusion of the old mindsets I held about my inadequacy. I felt compelled to dispel the illusion of deficiency in order to write this book.

Since I had been claiming to be an expert life coach, and I felt fraudulent, my pride prevented me from seeking help for my own despair and lack of passion. In the past I had experienced what I considered to be great expansions in spiritual awareness from my personal work with a few talented coaches. Somehow, I erroneously believed I had grown beyond needing a spiritual mentor or guru. But now in hiatus from my meditation group, I felt the need to find a new teacher, one who could point me in the right direction to attain peace of mind and restore my passion for meaningful living.

For a long time, I had been following Mooji, a Jamaican-born spiritual teacher and student of Papaji, (H. W. L. Poonja; a disciple of Ramana Maharshi), a teacher of non-duality, or Advaita Vedanta philosophy. I felt a special brotherhood, a cultural kinship with this African America man who shows up as spiritually awake. He is a model for me of someone who could passionately teach others true, authentic awakening, through the journey of SELF-awareness. I had been using many Mooji videos as instructional tools in my meditation groups, and appreciated how Mooji shared his loving wisdom and practical perspectives to guide others in awakening, And he did this with large groups from all over the world, via livestream and direct transmission from Portugal. However, although I admired Mooji and his teaching style, I certainly wasn't willing to travel to Portugal and sleep in a bunk bed to attend his silent retreat center, in order to meet him. I was just too sensible for that, or so I believed.

Therefore I was skeptical that meeting this famous guru at a big silent retreat held faraway in southern Portugal would have any more liberating impact on my state of mind, particularly since I had been reading his books and watching his videos for years. Weekly, on Sunday mornings, my wife, Jocelyn, and I would watch the Mooji videos from Monte Sahaja, Mooji's home and ashram in Portugal. I appreciated Mooji more as a skilled and awakened celebrity teacher whom I honored, not as a teacher that could coach me through my moments of despair.

The good news is that my wife isn't as practical as I am. For a while, she'd known that I was struggling emotionally and spiritually searching, so without even asking me, she purchased tickets for me to attend Mooji's retreat. Although I was apprehensive, this invitation to meet Mooji began to feel right, and eventually I looked forward to the proposed journey as an exciting adventure instead of a dreaded one.

Even though my enthusiasm was growing about visiting my YouTube guru, I usually do not enjoy long airplane trips, and this was going to be one; so when I thought about it, I was already experiencing deep resistance about traveling to Lisbon. I'm a pretty tall man, so fitting into a coach airplane seat can be challenging and sometimes painful. Since I thought I was traveling for the purpose of enlightenment, I decided I would stay open and not obsess too much about sitting in coach with my knees jammed in my chest for nine hours. I love meditation and was confident I could bliss out for at least two hours, but it was the other seven hours that troubled me.

This journey to the retreat started out dreadfully. I had planned to get to Lisbon a day early, giving me enough time to settle in and meet the special transportation Mooji provided to the retreat site at the Zmar Resort in southern Portugal. The first problem was that I couldn't get on the flight to Lisbon because my passport was going to expire in 6 months and I was stuck at a layover in Philadelphia. Airport management reassured me that I could spend the night in town and have my passport renewed the next day in downtown Philadelphia. But that would mean missing some of the retreat. Now the journey was starting to become an ordeal, and I was feeling overwhelmed and vulnerable. Even though I was apprehensive, I decided to miss the first day of the retreat to get my documents in order. I didn't like the idea of coming late but I forged ahead anyway, and the next day I was able to renew my passport and fly out that evening.

Once I got to Lisbon, I had to figure out how to get to the retreat center since I'd missed the courtesy bus. Speaking no Portuguese meant I had to depend on "Google translate" which can be useful, but is often inaccurate. I instinctively decided to take a public bus from the airport to a train terminal where I was originally supposed to board a courtesy bus to the center. But once I got to the train station the situation became even more confusing. No one seemed-to know where I was heading. The papers I'd printed were not helpful at all. And although everyone was kind, no one could tell me how to get there.

I showed a cab driver the address and he agreed to take me, but he let me know it would take about two hours and we would arrive in the middle of the day. Reluctantly, I agreed to this, despite the exorbitant fare. I felt greatly pressured to get there as soon as possible, so as not to miss another minute of the event. Even though I had to pay a small fortune for the trip, I was still enthusiastic about the journey ahead.

I finally arrived at the retreat in the middle of the second day, and because this was a silent event, no one spoke to me or even looked directly at me. This caused me to feel discouraged, isolated, and helpless. Because I was so late checking in, there was no one around at first and I had to drag my luggage all over the rocky campus until I found an administrator to assist me with housing.

But Mooji's back end administration was wonderful. The management updated me with all the information I'd missed during orientation the previous day, and assisted me in finding my cabin and helping with my bag. This cabin had two rooms and a bathroom. One of the rooms was tiny with only a double bed, and that was the luxury accommodation! My room was even smaller, with only a child-sized bunk bed with a wooden ladder. Since I was the last occupant to arrive to the room, I had no choice but to take the top bunk.

Once I climbed the ladder to the top bunk, I saw that my feet were going to hang over the end of this bed by at least two feet. Sleeping in that child-size bed with my feet dangling over the edge was incredibly uncomfortable and humbling. It seemed to me then that one of the important parts of this seven-day silent retreat was to be jolted out of my normal comfort zone, and I can testify to the discomfort.

The retreat was set up for an early morning and evening spiritual discourse, or *satsang,* with Mooji. The auditorium held over 800 devoted followers from around the world, with dozens of languages undergoing translation in real time through sophisticated audio equipment. In between events, wonderful Hindi devotional meditations, chanting, and kirtan music effectively kept my heart wide open each day.

But it was actually seeing Mooji in *satsang* every day that was the transformative experience for me. When I entered the auditorium, I would feel a peaceful presence almost immediately, and once Mooji entered the room, I became aware that my vibrational energy elevated significantly, throughout my body and whole being. I had always been cynical of the idea of "wholeness," but in Mooji's presence, I felt completely at home in his heart. This gentle-voiced, modest and loving man, exuding warmth and wisdom, was before me in the flesh! He delivered his message of self-discovery, higher power, and the road to conscious opening with so much tender encouragement and grace that we experienced him as a living mystic. Until then, I had never been exposed to such unconditional love and passionate joy.

Every day I watched his devoted followers fawn over him, pampering him with gifts, laying flowers at his feet with great affection, and I wondered if I could be bold enough just to shake his hand. However, I felt too timid to approach him.

In *satsang*, Mooji would speak on the unreliability of our illusory minds, urging us to leave past, future and present thoughts behind. He told us that only in the *Now* moment do we become witnesses to life in its perfection, free of all attachments, fears, and concerns. He said that staying present allows our vulnerable and wise hearts to be the source of our intelligence, and that by watching life unfold, moment by moment, we would always be freshly imbued with freedom, love, and overall, pure joy.

One morning at the end of *satsang*, I felt compelled to navigate through the crowd, and more toward the front of the auditorium just to get a closer look. For some reason one of the facilitators ushered me to the head of the line that had formed during the processional as Mooji was leaving the room.

All of a sudden, I was face to face with Mooji, and I wasn't sure how to respond. I felt sheepish but open, with an intense feeling of vulnerability. Suddenly, he walked right up to me and held out his arms for a hug, and I melted into his embrace. Tears flooded my eyes and I felt an incredible gratitude for the love he was extending to me. The only words that came to me were "thank you" and he replied simply with, "I love you". In that moment of surrender I was engulfed in his wholeness, feeling no boundary or separation between Mooji's heart and my own. I was simply lost in LOVE. As I composed myself with his intensity flowing organically through me, I watched him exit the building, and I suddenly became aware of a deeper awakening in my own self, an openness to—or an acceptance of—whatever was resonating inside my heart. Throughout that evening I began to experience waves of gratitude and harmony with all of my surroundings, including the way too small top bunk that I slept in. A different awareness of a greater capacity—the depth—of love in my heart that I now had to share, arose, and a sense of urgency to express that love toward others surged through me.

Once back home, I felt determination and excitement about finishing this book, but now my intention was deepened by an earnest and authentic passion for sharing truth. *Soul Power* was written to communicate the good news that openness to love can be nurtured, supported, and appreciated, that forgiveness is always self-forgiveness, and that love is both ubiquitous and eternal.

I hope that this book and the practices of SoulTranSync reveal to you your own soul journey of Awakening to your true Self.

Uncovering and Embracing

SOUL POWER

An Important Introduction to this Book and the SoulTranSync^{TM} Process

First let me state––and this is very important to know––*contentment and happiness do not need to be elusive.* I now understand this through my own experiences, study and teaching, but it took a while for me to believe it. You see, sustained happiness and peace of mind had always eluded me.

I grew up hoping for an upgraded version of myself to appear, especially since I felt and behaved like wounded prey. As an overweight and awkward boy, I was constantly bullied and teased. I spent my childhood feeling afraid, ashamed and worthless, but most of all misunderstood. My mother had no tolerance or understanding for this kind of weakness. She believed that black men should be strong and resilient, never showing vulnerability. Her practical but insensitive style of parenting only fueled my feelings of inadequacy.

By middle school I was struggling with reading, especially required group reading out loud. I felt terrified and panicked as I waited for my turn to read a paragraph of a book the class was reading. Not only did I freak out emotionally, but I would sweat profusely even before my turn. What made it worse was that other students looked forward to my breakdown.

One day a student humiliated me with his sarcasm about how he delighted in watching me read. Instead of ignoring him, I told him to "Kiss my ass." Although at that moment it felt amazing, and I felt justified for standing up for myself, the student threatened that he and his friends were going to fight me after school.

Believing I was in great danger, wanting to avoid him and protect myself from this humiliation, I went to the teacher for help. I was hoping she would rescue me from this bully's threat, but her only advice was to hide out in the classroom until they were gone. I spent the rest of that year hiding and running from that perceived beating, and I felt like a coward, or the expression that kids used back then, a "sissy."

By my late teens I learned to mask my insecurities by creating and promoting an aloof persona of confidence and control. Behind this super "cool" mask was the scared and defenseless little boy who just wanted approval, acceptance and respect from others.

As an adult maintaining this formidable façade was exhausting. Hiding behind a mask of strength became my full-time job. After a while, the philosophy of "Fake-it-'til-you-make-it" was basically my predominant outlook on life. I projected a compelling identity that was worthy and capable. But as this imposter, I suffered each day in a state of high anxiety coupled with the fear of exposure. Like many people who agonize with low self-esteem, I would often choose to live below my potential to avoid failure, or I would sell myself short by lowering expectations to avoid disappointment. I felt great shame about my fearfulness and feelings of inadequacy, hoping one day to become accomplished enough to no longer feel like a fraud. But acquiring more self-esteem would be a challenging, if not impossible endeavor, given what little I felt I had to work with. I was aware of my insufficiencies, but I also wanted to believe that there was relief from my suffering.

My Search Begins

By early adulthood, I learned in my search for answers that "Enlightenment" is a state where suffering doesn't exist, and bliss is eternally present.[1] Believing that this special state of being was attainable, I became a seeker of *nirvana* and a committed student of the practice of the *Law of Attraction*?. The Law of Attraction promised that I could gain control of my life by better managing my mind. Mind control made sense to me, since it was my mind that was suffering. But the disciplined practice of the Law of Attraction required vigilance and control over my mind that proved difficult. Over the years, I wrote and recited affirmations of empowerment, trying to reprogram my thinking. I read many books, learned numerous techniques, and practiced various meditation disciplines hoping to transcend my suffering. However, my efforts delivered little success.

As I got older, taking on a wife and children, career, community and financial success, my life became more complicated, and my low-level anxiety growled like a chained monster. A once courageous, resilient and high-energy person, I felt that I had become a wounded soul, and I anticipated that every day would bring me more pain and angst. I could feel myself contracting, and physical pain began to limit my mobility.

Like those with post-traumatic stress disorder (PTSD), intense, disturbing thoughts and feelings related to trauma that had long past invaded my mind and heart. I found myself reliving traumatic childhood events through distressing memories, flashbacks and emotions of sadness, fear or anger. I became detached and estranged from other people—even my close family and friends. I would often try to avoid situations or people that reminded me of difficult events, yet, even beyond this, I found myself experiencing strong negative reactions to regular and ordinary life challenges. I needed relief from such a painful existence, and longed to find that high self-esteem I sought and occasionally had felt as a child.

I endlessly searched like a wounded animal for relief from my pain. All my psychology and self-help books, training and empowerment workshops seemed unable to console me or diminish my disappointments.

One afternoon I was sitting at my favorite Starbucks reading Eckhart Tolle's masterful book *The New Earth,* and in that moment, I was feeling open and available to a deeper understanding of my life. I had been struggling in my business, and my mind was full of confusion. How was I going to pay my staff at the Chartered school I was responsible for? How was I going to create a functioning environment that inspired commitment to the work we were doing? How was I going to survive making some very hard decisions that had to be made?

While sipping my warm latte I came across this line in Tolle's book, "The primary cause of unhappiness is never the situation, but your thoughts about it. Be aware of the thoughts you are thinking".[1] Wow! In that moment I deeply received what Mr. Tolle was pointing to, and I felt the book was speaking personally to my heart, sharing with me a truth that I had persistently avoided. The message was that it was essential that I be aware of the thoughts I was thinking, and I had an *Ah ah* moment when I realized how I was always judging myself for these thoughts. These judgments were heavy, unforgiving, and rather dark interpretations of my life, often brought on by dread and self-incrimination.

I understood in that moment that choosing to be aware of my thoughts meant acknowledging everything I might falsely believe. This was BIG. But healing would take a new type of courage that I wasn't sure I had. The courage I needed required no effort, but it did require the willingness to ask the questions, "What am I believing?" and "Is it true?" The more I called my beliefs "true" the more miserable I was. I realized that *because I had been unwilling to inquire about such painful and limiting thoughts, I continued to support them in tormenting me.* This sudden awareness ignited my passion and commitment to myself to inquire and accept only the truth, in a deeper, more profound way.

This defining moment altered my point of view of how I would now relate to myself knowing I needed to take full responsibility for my inner world: what I am feeling or resisting. Moreover, I had to inquire about what I am unconsciously attached to, which is not easily accessible. But I could work backwards from the conscious feelings, inquiring and speculating about what my unconscious mind might be implying.

Ever since that moment, I no longer believe that my "mind" is outside my ability to regulate the way I think as long as I grow in awareness, and as a result, true freedom to experience my life in its fullness is now possible. With this new directive I am able to explore my self with insight and kindness toward "me" and my "Self." This is how the *SoulTranSync*™ (Soul Transcendence Synchronization) practice was born.

Self-Awareness as a Key to Self-Acceptance

My life expanded once I surrendered to myself. That might sound vague and confusing, so allow me to explain a little further. I have learned that the only thing that truly matters in life is how I relate to myself. Through practiced Self-Awareness I no longer believe that anything exists outside of my own perception and that my only responsibility is to my perception of myself and not to the objects that appear or disappear in my consciousness.

This book illustrates how I loved, cared for, and nurtured myself, mirroring to you, the reader, the quality of my experiences on the path to spiritual alignment, while focusing on "Awareness;" the agent of change was *Awareness.* This I know for sure.

When we begin to realize that we are a spiritual beings having human experiences, our minds take on expanded awareness. To expand our human awareness and heal contracted personal perspectives, we first align with and adjust our limited view of self to include something larger, our Self with a capital S, the larger understanding of our relationship to the universe overall. Later I'll explore with you the three possibilities of SELF.

Why I Wrote this Book and How to Use It

You will find as you read this book, that my personal story of the journey to Self-Awareness is offered as a context for how this process has transformed my own life. Childhood trauma, and the need for self-protection, gave rise to a repetitive program of negative beliefs that kept me locked in a cycle of despair. My desperation finally led me to the creation of the *SoulTranSync*™ process and practices.

I don't believe that my personal history is unique or special, but I am now aware that my story provides a perfect model for the way our minds can cause us ceaseless suffering. Habitual thinking and my relentless tale convinced me that I was always wrong, or "not enough," as a person. My mind perfectly replicated stories and perceptions that supported and entrenched limiting beliefs of unworthiness in my psyche. I wrote this book as a way to reach others with the good news, that there is a way to free ourselves from the tyranny of our minds, and to live from our hearts as well.

It is my intention to pass on to you the simple tools and practices I used to free myself from many of my beliefs about happiness. In writing this book I had to examine how all those perceptions were tainted with a shadowy overlay that sabotaged any chance of success or healing. My personal story of the journey to Self-Awareness is woven throughout the book to assist you as the reader in discovering how the *SoulTranSync™* process changed my entire life for the better.

Each Soul has the capacity to transcend the past *and awaken to the present moment.* The implementation of this innovative teaching, that I've named *SoulTranSync™* (STS), accelerates Soul evolution. SoulTranSync is intended as a useful foundation for preparing us to renovate and ultimately strengthen the relationship with the one being we truly long to know intimately: Our Self.

I wrote *Uncovering and Embracing Soul Power* in Four Parts in a format that supports your progressive understanding of the major concepts. Once read, you may choose to revisit certain sections and chapters out of sequence to deepen the heart's understanding of Soul Transcendence. Additional material, exercises and practices can be found in the *SoulTranSync™* Workbook, which you may order through the website, **www.SoulTranSync.com**

The SoulTranSync Process

As I began my soul journey, I explored a system that incorporates powerful practices and key elements into the SoulTranSync Process. STS consists of the Core Practices—Non-Duality, Self-Inquiry and Forgiveness using the Hawaiian tradition Ho'oponopono. These concepts are essential for understanding and embracing your Soul Power. Woven within these practices are the Core Elements of Acceptance, Gratitude and Forgiveness, which broaden your transformational experience.

The SoulTranSync Core Practices and Elements are explained and discussed—along with my personal journey as a guide for you—in the Four Parts of this book.

- Part One acquaints you with the meaning of SoulTranSync and the concept of Non-Duality, a philosophy that acknowledges our non-separation or oneness with all that exists. With this understanding, Non-Duality expands our consciousness, altering our perceptions to greater expressions of love and peace.
- Part Two explores the many facets of Awareness using the effective tool of Self-Inquiry, a questioning technique, to help us realize our true nature. As we cultivate awareness of our various emotional states, we gain a stronger command of our behaviors and lay the groundwork for Soul Transcendence.
- Part Three describes each of the previously mentioned Core Elements — Acceptance, Gratitude and Forgiveness. These are the fundamental elements for living a life of Grace, Infinite Love, Mercy, Favor, and Goodwill.

- Finally, Part Four interprets the forgiveness practice of Ho'oponopono, and how forgiveness can heal ideas of separation bringing inner peace. This ageless Hawaiian practice originally designed to "make things right," encourages us to clean and clear any thoughts, perceptions or beliefs that limit us from uncovering and embracing our inner Soul Power.

SoulTranSync elicited major transformative changes in my outlook, and gave me a more potent understanding of my original and innocent nature. I believe that these practical approaches to Self-Awareness represent the "best practices" for seekers looking for a simple, direct approach out of their suffering mind into acceptance and awareness.

By integrating all these powerful methods for Self-Awareness into one ground-breaking practice, *SoulTranSync™ (STS)* transforms the heart and enables each of us to fully embrace our Soul Power.

My Discovery and Soul Journey

I wrote *Uncovering and Embracing Soul Power* to share my journey of awakening to Self-Love within me, but also to impart a creative, inspired, and transformative practice for eliminating suffering—a remedy for the lack of self-worthiness, for anyone who is ready to receive this information.

All Suffering is Resistance or Non-acceptance

How we relate to our lives determines the quality of our experiences. I have learned that once our tender innocent hearts are wounded, only self-love and true self-acceptance can heal them. When we are hurting we are resisting life; we are not accepting *what is*. We need to determine what is real and what is just a **story** made up of negative thoughts. When using the words "story" or "stories", I'm speaking to the narrative or storyline that our minds will create in an attempt to describe or explain ***what is.*** We all bear traumas or difficulties, and we can heal from them. But how do we learn to love ourselves when there is no one to teach us?

I had to accept that it was my heart that was broken, not my mind. If I was to find Self-Love, I needed a path back to my innocent self, back to my SOUL. The soul work that I began exploring was a dramatic change from the reprogramming practices of the Law of Attraction that I had initially believed would be my salvation.

I have now changed the direction of my seeking from the external world to my own compassionate heart. I realized that my mind had been programmed with a tremendous amount of judgment, and that clinging to these judgments was a life-sentence I had imposed upon myself, in a way, it was my "addiction." Only through a soul journey or through Soul Transcendence, would I be free to transform and experience the happiness I sought. I realized I could help others—with similar feelings and situations—to experience self-love and true joy. In this book, *Uncovering and Embracing Soul Power*, I share with you my path to freedom through enlightenment. I now know that enlightenment is not acquired through effort, but through *intent,* and that the real objective of enlightenment is absolute awareness and acceptance of our true nature.

But perhaps equally important has been the recognition of how continual stories are created through our distorted perceptions.

True healing can happen by cultivating genuine love, compassion and forgiveness for ourselves through the tenderness of our own hearts. This is what I call **Soul Power**, and this new enlightened relationship with one's self is the beautiful fruit nurtured to maturity through the practice of ***SoulTranSync***™ (STS).

SoulTranSync™ is a most innovative practice; however it is supported by both ancient and multi-cultural tools and techniques. Although ***SoulTranSync*** utilizes mystical and spiritual principles, it is not a religious technique per se, but rather a practice for everyone regardless of one's faith or belief systems. It inspires in us a unique transformative process that shifts us from resistance into spiritual alignment. By accepting and using the inspiring ideals and practices of *SoulTranSync™,* we are empowered to flow effortlessly in a more dynamic, heartful, and open existence.

The Logic of SoulTranSync™

Doesn't it make sense to become aware of and tap into our Souls? Being in continual communion with your own soul is the most important practice of spiritual alignment, and the only true pathway to self-realization. It is often believed that self-realization requires becoming a new, improved, or better person, but realization is about becoming the person we were meant to be, and the person we already are, but don't yet know how to be. Self-realization is nothing more than the vigilant conscious awareness of Self. Attaining awareness of this important concept enables us to obtain true freedom and self-empowerment.

A Meaningful New Existence

Many of us live lives that lack contentment and fulfillment because we feel as though they are without meaning. The *STS* practice prepares us for a meaningful new existence that leaves our hearts open to spontaneous miracles, passionate love, increased productivity and the natural flow of abundance. The practice offers a fearless and nurturing way of living not only for our selves, but for humanity. By learning that our own heart has intelligence, wisdom and spiritual insight, we become open to compassion, empathy and intimacy with all living beings. *STS* is a practice of consciously eliminating the resistance in our minds and letting go of memories that are problematic, unloving, or not in our best interest.

Coming from the Heart Changes Your Life

As we become heart-driven and heart-centered, instead of mind-driven and obsessed, the practice reveals our authentic purpose. Knowing our life's meaning and direction is more than discovering which career to follow or what job to take. Having the "right purpose" for our life engenders healthy relationships, harmonious surroundings, and inspiring lifestyles.

Discovering our authentic and higher *Self* highlights just how important and essential we are to the world. The truth is, this world wouldn't exist without us perceiving it. And how we perceive it, creates our experience in it.

Your Perception is the Script for the Movie of your Life

The screenplay has a writer, an editor, and a director who is also you. As the director of your life, you are self-empowered. Self-empowerment means giving yourself permission to accept life on its own grounds, even when disorder and messiness are present.

Even within the chaos, life is constantly revealed to us in perfect order, whether we realize it or not. Perfect order doesn't mean how we may want our lives to unfold. The wanting of anything feeds illusions of lack and limitation. Self-empowerment means we can stand amidst our own creation and not be victimized by its appearance.

As whole self-empowered beings, we are aware that nothing could ever be insufficient or missing. People, problems and change show up exactly as they are meant to for our conscious evolution. Growth or expansion is never as neat and tidy as we might think or want. Any resistance in our mind and body to our story plot is just that, resistance, not for us to be bothered by it, not for us to endure it, but only for us to become aware of it, so then we can let it go.

STS practice teaches us to live in the moment and trust life with an open heart. When we choose to stay peaceful and receptive in our thinking, even if we forget and find ourselves having pessimistic thoughts or bad memories, we can immediately surrender into conscious presence, or spacious awareness. Conscious presence holds the awareness in the moment that frees us from identification with any untrustworthy thought or emotion.

Spacious awareness, or having an open perspective, is void of judgment and evaluation. Only Love exists in this space. Once spacious awareness is made known to us, Soul Transcendence or soul alignment is experienced in acts of love from a heart full of forgiveness and over-flowing with gratitude.

With this book, *Uncovering and Embracing Soul Power,* we can begin that ongoing soul journey to self-empowerment and a more fulfilling existence. With practice, using this *SoulTranSync™* system will take you home to your True Self where contentment and happiness reside. Here is something, after all my years of struggling, that finally was successful for me, and I'm convinced STS will work for you too. Thank you for turning the page and joining me in beginning this exciting and fulfilling *SoulTranSync*™ journey together!

Uncovering and Embracing Soul Power

SoulTranSync™

PART ONE

AWARENESS AND UNDERSTANDING

It is all Awareness and cannot be known.

~ H.W.L. Poonja (Papaji)

CHAPTER 1

A NEW RELATIONSHIP WITH OURSELVES

In the first five chapters of Part One of this book we explore Awareness and the philosophical understanding that we are all individual (self) manifestations of one SELF, and that we are connected through our embodied Aware or True Self, in powerful ways.

The success of using my signature process SoulTranSync™ depends in great measure upon the level of apprehension of the larger field of Awareness, which can be brought at any given moment, and moment by moment, to the perception of our self.

In Part One we discover the meaning of *SoulTranSync™* (STS) and how using it leads to a new relationship with ourselves. We present as well, the concepts of the Soul and Soul Transcendence along with notions of the aspects of self, Self and SELF, all seen through the vehicle of Awareness. As these ideas are revealed and discussed, we are led deeper into the discovery of Self-Realization. Part One also provides vital information about our delusions, our shadows, our egos, and how we synchronize with the Self. In the process we learn about how the ego is transformed through the Aware Ego Process into the Aware, or True Self.

The rest of Part One discusses the Wounded Inner Child and my own story as examples of awakening from the pain and suffering of negative beliefs, and the process I used in order to heal and transform my life.

Woven throughout Part One are the ways that the *SoulTranSync*™ (STS) process has transformed my life. By presenting my personal story and path to awakening, I have created a template for us to follow. As I remember the anxious young person I used to be, I am amazed at the peace I now have, my improved feelings of self-worth, my success, and the joy I feel and express today. *This can happen for you too.*

When we begin the practice of *SoulTranSync*™ (STS) we pledge ourselves to a unique transformative process that can shift us from resistance into spiritual alignment. Soul-Tran-Sync means "Soul Transcendence in Synchronization", or more simply put, divine spiritual alignment through awareness. In this alignment we are able to discover freedom from all suffering, peace of mind, and the awareness that anything we could ever imagine is already ours.

For the sake of the STS practice, the word 'soul' is best interpreted by writer, Gary Zukav, the author of *The Seat of the Soul.* In it he writes that "the Soul is that part of you that existed before you were born and that will exist after you die."[2] It's the highest, most noble part of ourselves. Spiritual teacher Deepak Chopra wrote that the Soul is "the core of our being." [3] It is eternal. It doesn't exist in space/time. It's a field of infinite possibilities, infinite creativity. It's an internal reference point with which we can always be in touch.

Participating in continual communion with our own Soul is the most important practice of spiritual alignment, and the truest pathway to self-realization. *Self-realization* is the knowing that we are one with the presence of God everywhere, and that God's omnipresence is our omnipresence. We are just as much a part of God now as we will ever be, and all we need do is expand our knowing of this truth through awareness.

It is often believed that Self-realization requires becoming a new, improved, or better person, but realization is about becoming that person you were meant to be, which as I said in my introduction, you already are, but don't yet know how to be. Self is the unconditioned nature of who we are, that acts as a kind of facilitator between our ego identity (self) and our higher awareness (Self). Self-realization is nothing more than the *vigilant conscious awareness of Self.*

The STS practice prepares us for a meaningful new existence that leaves our hearts open to spontaneous miracles and to passion for what and who we love. At the same time, our lives open to inspired productivity and the natural flow of abundance. The practice offers a fearless and nurturing way of living not only for our selves, but for all humanity. By learning that our unique heart has intelligence, wisdom and spiritual insight, we become available to experience compassion, empathy, and intimacy, with all living beings. STS is a practice of consciously releasing feelings associated with past negative experiences that produce habitual negative thoughts while anticipating events that have not yet even occurred. This technique eliminates the resistance in our minds, and in turn, helps us let go of memories that are not loving, not in our best interest, or problematic.

As we become heart-driven and heart-centered, as opposed to mind-driven and obsessed, the practice reveals our authentic life's purpose. Knowing our life's purpose is more than discovering which career to follow or job to take. *Right purpose*, or what can be called "being in alignment with our authentic nature," will engender truer relationships and more harmonious contexts. Ultimately, we begin living a lifestyle that can be inspirational to ourselves and others.

Discovering our authentic Self highlights just how important and essential each of us is to the world. Each one of us is unique and has our own perceptions of the world. And the truth is our perceptions of the world create its existence and these perceptions can become projections to write the stories of our lives. Our screenplays have writers, editors, and directors, all of whom are also us.

As directors, we are *Self-empowered*. Even when life is not going our way, it is still unfolding in perfect order, whether we realize it or not. Perfect order doesn't mean how we might want our life to be or to look. Self-empowerment means we can stand in the midst of our own creation as it is unfolding, without becoming victimized by its appearance.

As *Self*-empowered beings we become aware that nothing could ever be insufficient or missing. People, problems and change will show up exactly as they are meant to for our conscious evolution. Growth or expansion is never as neat and tidy as we might think. Any resistance in our mind and body to our story plot is just that—resistance. It's not for us to be bothered by it; nor is it to be endured, but we must become aware of it, so that then—we can let it go.

STS practice teaches us to live in the moment and trust life with an open heart. We may choose to stay peaceful and receptive in our thinking. However, if we forget and get caught in pessimistic thoughts or bad memories, we can immediately surrender into a more spacious awareness. Conscious presence, then, can embrace an awareness in the moment that frees us from identification with any awkward or sticky thought or emotion.

Spacious awareness means having an open perspective that is vast, and void of judgment and limiting evaluation. Only love exists in this space. Once *spaciousness* is made known to us, soul transcendence or soul alignment is experienced in acts of love, from a heart of forgiveness and over-flowing gratitude. We can then call this *spaciousness,* "Awareness," with a capital 'A.'

The *SoulTranSync*™ (STS) practice focuses on our heart's qualities of intuition and knowing, (not on our thinking), to encourage our understanding and discernment about life and all of its mysteries. Also inherent in STS is the awareness that our heart is the Heart of the World, and that as we heal, grow and change, our planet evolves, as does every living being on it.

In discovering this natural heart-driven alignment, a new relationship with our selves is born. This relationship is a key to the transformative experience of the SoulTranSync practice and essential for self-realization.

In addition, this age is now one of a greater expansion in Consciousness and is engaging human beings in accepting the idea that we are perfect and whole just as we are, that no insufficiency or inadequacy actually exists. Understanding and trusting that in every moment, life is presenting to us all we need to navigate the sometimes-tumultuous world we live in, is the way of spiritual alignment, and the centerpiece of *SoulTranSync*™.

CHAPTER 2

WHAT IS SOUL TRANSCENDENCE AND THE SELF?

Outside of all the activities of this life, beyond successes and failures, relationships and acquisitions, there is the Soul. That Soul is the spiritual part of a person or self, that spark of light that is believed to give life to the body.

We have within ourselves the potential for total Awareness and Self-realization, through what I am calling Soul Transcendence. Soul Transcendence is the process of elevating our awareness beyond our body, mind and emotions, and awakening to the conscious Awareness of our Self—who we truly are. By establishing Soul consciousness, we are no longer bound or limited by this world, nor by our identification with it, but rather we can experience and express more of the qualities of our Self—love, peace, joy, wisdom, compassion, and abundance.

Soul Transcendence offers an approach to Self-realization that centers on a multidimensional Soul Awareness. This Awareness becomes incorporated into our everyday life, in tangible, practical ways, letting us align more and more with our Soul. We increasingly live from that alignment.

The direct result of Soul Transcendence is that we perpetually rise above situations and see our lives from a loving point of view. Soul Transcendence uncovers our hearts and reveals to us a more spacious perspective, beyond our minds, stories of fear, limitations and judgments of insufficiency.

Because the Transcendent Soul moves in and out of linear time as it evolves, it depends on the limited mind or "self'" to give name and meaning to life, actually causing us to forget the truth of Self. But either gradually or suddenly as our souls evolve, we begin to remember our greater alignment as the Self and our oneness with all life. Soul Transcendence is the journey to discover the "I Am" Self through the experiencing of life.

Therefore, before we dive headlong further into Understanding and Embracing Soul Power, let's examine the three aspects of *"self" which are: self/Self/SELF*

What is the self/Self/SELF?

self

The traditional concept of 'self' defines the conditions of identity that make one subject of experience separate from all others; this involves understanding the nature of personal identity. For example, "I am me, and I do this, and I don't do that. I have this job, I'm married to this person, I like these things . . . " This viewpoint makes the human perspective of individual existence separate from other aspects of creation. Many refer to the self with a lowercase s as "ego," or who I think I am. Ego, often identified as the "self," is generally referred to as our physical world identity structure that is necessary to think, operate, make decisions and take action in the physical world. Ego identity includes our physical bodies as well as our minds, our names, our careers, our nationali ties, our sexual identities, our personalities, our affinities and preferences, our beliefs, plus any other descriptive features of human identity.

Ego-identity thoughts promote the illusion of a separate self, where we consider ourselves separate entities, located in, and as, our bodies. The world teaches us that every person we meet is an ego-centered being as well, possessing his or her own 'mind,' with his or her own thoughts and consciousness.

As part of the Collective Consciousness (the consciousness of all humans throughout history), our ego selves also possess all individual human characteristics included in the physical universe.

Self

The *Self with a capital S is* not engrossed in the ego's urgency, combativeness and emotional reactions; instead, it gives us a dispassionate, detached and transcendent overview of our selves and our lives.

The embodied Self is transcendent when it encompasses the Soul. According to Jungian psychology, the Self includes all the elements of the human soul including the ego, the conscious mind, the personal subconscious, the collective unconscious and all other elements of our psychological being.

By embracing stronger and broader identification with the Self, our transcendent souls broaden in Awareness. A greater awareness becomes apparent as we acquire more profound understanding of our Soul's journey. This is because the Self holds an overview of the transcending Soul, free from the ego's distortions, fear of our shadows, judgments, misperceptions and delusions.

As Self, your mind and my mind are connected to a universal mind that encompasses the consciousness of all humans. In this aspect of the greater SELF, or "Self," we no longer cling to our judgments and limited perspectives that create our individual problems and perpetuate suffering.

SELF

As human beings, we have certain emotions, thoughts, and behaviors in common. However, while we may know sensations or feelings of sadness, we are not unhappiness. We may know our beliefs of unworthiness or disillusionment, but we can never be "not enough." No thoughts, feelings, appearances, activities or judgments are real within the Awareness of SELF. Our essential nature, SELF, is perfect, without personal attributes, and therefore identity-less, complete as it is, pure spaciousness itself, filled with a vast undisturbed peace that cannot be diluted or divided. SELF is that unembodied infinite energy field that we liken to "God."

The Aware or True Self

Regardless of our paths, backgrounds, or religious influences, ultimately, as seekers, we search for ideals and descriptions that point to the original nature of our True Self, and it is a direct experience of that Self that we pursue. By aligning with the "One who is aware" or the Aware Self, we are naturally poised to explore the truth of who we are, and who we are not; and through inquiry, in evitably, we can arrive at the realization of our true nature as Self.

To receive the liberating and transformative effects from the Soul-TranSync practice, there is one fundamental requirement needed: *re-imagining our s/Self-identity.* Choosing to relate to our selves as Conscious Awareness is a critical element of Soul Transcendence. This relationship with our Selves is essential for the evolution of our Soul, and manifesting enlightened change in our lives.

> *By envisioning the Self, we can expand our limited perspectives about who we truly are and merge with better aligned and more spacious perspectives of human awareness and experiences.*

The fundamental awareness that arises from inquiry is the discovery, "I am not the "I-thought" that I believe myself to be." All personal beliefs and the emotions that are generated and inspired by the "I" are fundamentally delusions or false identities. The only authentic way out of this mistaken idea of our existence is self-inquiry, or asking the question, "Who is the I that believes this thought, or feels this way?" Inquiry challenges the mistaken belief that this I, the one we constantly repeat inside our minds, is the truth of who we are. This simple and direct investigation is said to be the most direct path to realizing the true Aware Self.

The SELF is that field of transcendent, unchanging, unlimited, persevering and pervasive elements brought into our awareness as that all-knowing aspect of ourselves, through the Self. The Self contains objectivity and is wide open to accept everything, and, therefore, excludes nothing. Everything is allowed; everything is permitted within the Self. The Self encompasses all individual viewpoints, including contradictory feelings and impulses, accepting both the sinner and the saint as one expression of the wholeness of life within the field of Self.

CHAPTER 3

ABOUT AWARENESS

You are the unchangeable Awareness
in which all activity takes place.[4]

~ H. W.L. Poonja (Papaji)

Awareness is the cornerstone of the SoulTranSync (STS) paradigm and the most important ally for expanding consciousness. Awareness is necessary to explore the SoulTranSync Core Practices and Elements found in Parts Two and Three of this book. Awareness is our ability to directly *know and perceive* life unfolding, moment by moment. Conscious awareness describes our ability to be aware of our self (i.e. self-awareness), including our thoughts, sensations, perceptions and core beliefs. As Awareness evolves it reveals to us our multidimensional true nature, and we begin to discover subtler emotional layers within us, along with our heart's expanded capacity to feel and recognize them.

Because the vastness of Awareness holds all knowledge and unlimited possibilities, its gifts are generally only revealed to our limited minds over time. The mind's reliance on time and its belief in a separate Self limit our access to the gifts of ever-expanding and ever-present Awareness. As we continue to grow in our Awareness, we tend to experience its delicious fruit more frequently, its greater love and peaceful understanding. Most notably, Awareness can transform ordinary problematic thinking into extraordinary insights and opportunities, through softening the mind's need to cling to knowledge. Expanded awareness allows us to stay-open and fluid to life as it unfolds, weighing and exploring opposite viewpoints for fresher, more inclusive solutions to the appearance of life's challenges.

Becoming more "aware" of Awareness creates subtle but notable and perceptive shifts in the ways we see others, enabling us to interact in the world with greater compassion and patience. As we empathize with those who suffer, we are also inspired to attempt to ease their pain with kindness and gestures of love. What we call our ego begins to melt away, and we behave less selfishly, from inspiration and the experience of fulfillment. With this more expanded point of view, we witness ourselves connecting better with others and having deeper relationships with those we love.

As we become more aware, we begin to notice our willingness to truly love ourselves, warts and all. Awareness eventually exposes us to our self-criticism and those judgments we have about our thoughts and actions. By freeing ourselves of these inner criticisms, we begin to change the way we think and behave, and we can enjoy a richer life, better aligned with our soul desires.

I realize that the pursuit of greater awareness, or "spiritual awakening," can often be a challenging and lonely or solitary journey. It requires a commitment to exploring our deepest self: our Soul. It forces us to turn inward to listen to our heart and its inner wisdom.

Awareness helps peel back the problem-filled layers of mind, like stripping off the outer layers of an onion, to reveal the potential options, possibilities, and solutions to our daily challenges.

As these outer layers are removed, we have greater access to our heart's real desires, those that include broader insight and wisdom into our stories of conditional love. Awareness brings us more awareness and the capacity to tap into our vulnerable but wise hearts, where we can hear the voice of our deeper Selves, telling us to *Love*—and only love.

CHAPTER 4

THE SHADOW, MISGUIDED THOUGHTS, AND SYNCHRONIZING WITH THE SELF

Just as a candle cannot burn without fire,
men cannot live without a spiritual life.

~ *Buddha*

Awareness always reveals to us peaceful, more encouraging points of view about what appears to be happening in our lives. The discovery of fresher perspectives shifts how we engage and show up in our life experiences. With these new aware points of view, a more detached objectivity toward our selves replaces those older, narrower, conditional or judgmental ideas of who we are.

Self-aware detachment does not mean a withdrawal from life, but actually engages life more robustly with heartfelt passion. In this way the Self is able to include all opposing traits in our personas, as well as the contrary or disowned ones that we cast into *shadow*. Less loved aspects, taken collectively, might be called the *Shadow-self*.

Our vulnerability is often *disowned*, suppressed, judged, and we unconsciously refuse to acknowledge it. With Self-awareness, this feeling of vulnerability can finally be embraced and integrated as intrinsic to the fullness of being human. Our multidimensional nature, then, no longer has to be divided into our good qualities and bad qualities. Instead, all human qualities are included within the wholeness of one's Self.

Like most people I adamantly avoided vulnerability. I now understand that in order to be vulnerable, I have to be okay with all of me, and not just the admirable and optimistic qualities of my personality. This means I must accept the parts of me that I don't want to see, and those parts of me that I certainly don't want others to know exist. Even if I do not exactly 'love' those less-attractive qualities, I can allow them the space to co-exist.

The *Shadow* is the part of us that is not shiny, pretty or fun. It reveals what we deny or keep hidden from other people, and grows by our negative self-talk, or what we think about ourselves that we don't like. We all do this to some extent. As an example, you probably have never said to a friend, "Although I appear supportive, I'm really jealous of your success and can't wait for you to fail." We keep those thoughts about ourselves hidden, along with anything else we do not like to think, much less allow anyone else to know about ourselves. Even worse, we repress those negative thoughts and can project them onto others. But greater awareness can prevent those potential tinder boxes of condemnation.

Me, Myself, and the Delusion of TRUE

Suffering is most often generated by continually taking on false identities that are not loving or in our best interests. For example, if I failed at a goal or a dream that I badly wanted, I might say to myself "I am not good enough" or "I am a failure." These are completely erroneous beliefs and can't be empirically "TRUE." For thoughts to be TRUE they would have to be irrefutable, impossible to deny or disprove. Therefore, when I refer to myself as insufficient, I am denying the SELF, which is empty of judgment and perfect as it is. Abiding as the 'Self' as described above and in Chapter 3, I do not need to do anything to improve it or to make it better. But as an "I-thought," I might obsess over the imperfection perceived, personalizing the belief instead of letting it pass.

It is our misdirected thinking that causes our mind to call a mistaken belief, TRUE. Once the mind accepts something about us to be TRUE, it's game over, because we can easily become stuck in a certainty about ourselves that is unloving and judgmental. And there is no easy way out of it, either. The belief becomes viral, almost like an organism feeding on sugar to keep it alive. Like sugar, it can also become an addiction.

By accepting a belief as TRUE, our minds go on autopilot. They continually look for evidence to support what we have accepted as TRUE. We carry this false identity around with us, refusing to put it down, no matter how painful. We compulsively repeat the lie over and over to our selves until we completely identify with it and believe that lie is who we are.

This kind of circular thought is exhausting and undermines self-esteem. We ask ourselves questions that repeatedly send us back to that same divisive mindset for our answers, where there is no relief. The questions are always a harsh dead end. For example, our minds will habitually choose a closed qualifying question, similar to, "Is something wrong with me?" that has a Yes/No response. As a judgmental question, it is inevitably followed by other pointless questions like, "How did I get myself into this situation?" or "How can I get what I want?" Or, "What is it going to cost me?" Finally, we may ask, "Why do I always end up here?" Or, "Why does this always happen to me?" The mind loves these questions like a dog loves a bone, because they give the mind something to chew on, believe in, or try to substantiate.

Synchronizing with the Self

Through stronger and broader identification with the Self, our transcendent souls grow in awareness and our perceptions evolve. Increasingly novel and aware changes in perception become more visible to ourselves when we acquire a greater, more significant understanding of the Soul's journey. This is because the Self has an overview of the transcending Soul, free from the ego's distortions, fear of our shadows, judgments, misperceptions and delusions.

Instead, of those negativities, we identify and synchronize with the Self as it is infused with Awareness rather than the egotistical self ("me") and are able to produce valuable benefits for our lives. We call this aware-infused Self our *Aware Self.* These benefits include better management of those shadow identities and a loosening of our psychological battles with the ego.

By expanding our identity through this reflective process of Awareness of our Self and our Soul's journey, we encourage a peaceful resolve for whatever divisiveness appears in front of us. "Reality" is always perfect because it's "what is," and not some perceived, often limited, interpretation of life. Spiritual awakening can't occur without first observing our beliefs and dissolving whatever untruths we find.

> *It is only our ignorance or lack of awareness of who we are that causes us to suffer.*

From an Aware Self to an Aware Ego

Accepting the possibility that there can be an "Aware Self" with which to synchronize, we can predict the eventuality of an "Aware Ego."

Thus, if we have become aware of *Self* as the spaciousness in which this life as "self" is embodied, then we can adopt a conscious aware "self-identity" that begins with a choice to be aligned with our "Aware Self."

In adopting an aware identification with *Self,* we begin to align with "Reality" through our *Self,* as the witnessing "self" progresses. As we synchronize more fully with this witness, we learn more about how to live our lives through the Self instead of a lower ego-identified self ("me".) By realizing this perspective, we become more skillful and experience valuable benefits to our lives.

These new benefits include both better management of shadow identities sometimes referred to in this book as *Disowned Identities (DI)* and a loosening of our psychological battles with the "ego." This ego is basically a mechanism for protection, for choosing either flight or fight responses as an example, and we complicate its purpose and instill it with ideas and identifications that create pain and suffering for us.

As previously discussed, *Disowned Identities* or *shadows* represent the aspects of our personality and ego that are either denied or overlooked, and generally rejected by our conscious mind. We all identify with and cling to stories of who we like to believe ourselves to be, but as a multidimensional Self, nothing is disallowed, including our *shadow*. We can be aware of it but give it no energy and forgive its neurosis.

The following are two examples of the way Soul Transcendence expands our identity and encourages peaceful resolution through greater awareness of "what is" or what can be referred to as "Reality." Reality is always the state of the objective world as it actually exists, as opposed to an idealistic or an imagined idea of it. Reality, therefore, can be defined as Absolute, as Self-sufficient, and not subject to human decisions or conventions.

Example 1:

> Although I sometimes suffer when my children don't respect my boundaries (**a *disowned identity (DI)*** or victim perspective), I am aware that that interpretation isn't true. ***In Reality nothing of this nature is true as Self.*** My children are only reflecting back to me my own rebellious character and resistance to authority. This would be an *aware* transcendent perspective.

And Example 2:

> Although I didn't get the job opportunity I believed I was most qualified for (**a *disowned identity (DI)*** or victim perspective), it wasn't offered to me. **In Reality as Self I am never denied or rejected.** I'm open to receive my opportunity in perfect timing. Again, this is *an aware transcendent perspective.*

So as the Self, we are always aligned with Reality and its perfection, and once this becomes second-nature to us, the Aware Self can inform, educate, develop, and direct an Aware Ego.

CHAPTER 5

SOUL TRANSCENDENCE AND THE AWARE EGO USING THE AWARE EGO PROCESS

We don't see things as they are; we see them as we are.[5]

~ Aniäs Nin

This process of evolving our Soul through the Aware Ego is essential to the SoulTranSync practice and to how the Soul can transcend the illusion of ego by synchronizing with the Self.

Now that we can accept the notion of an Aware Ego, we can postulate an Aware Ego Process.

> *The Aware Ego Process is not a sequential step by step practice, but an amorphous realization or awareness of our energetic states of being.*

The Aware Ego Process (AEP) assists us in merging ego and Soul into an expanded and ever-evolving awareness of Self and moves us towards genuine positive changes in our outlook and behavior. The AEP helps us to evolve our soul's awakening to the Infinite within our current finite state of being, allowing us to experience our Soul in all its varied expressions when we are in pain, in need, in trouble, through when we feel good and want to increase our joyful connectedness to each other and the world.

How does this happen?

"POES" and More on "DI"

Ego, Collective Consciousness and Primary Operating Ego Structure ("POES")

The ego believes in the illusion of a separate self, in which we consider our "self" as an individual person who is a separate entity, located in, responding through, and identified with, and as, a body. This illusion—that we are the body—is at the core of all suffering, encouraging us to protect and defend something that doesn't exist, while creating intoxicating stories that we react to and believe, which are not TRUE. Unaware egos wage war with phantom opponents and distract us from the truth of who we really are.

Identities

An Unaware Ego is concerned with survival and is constantly in fear, while an Aware Ego is focused on service, and is grounded in love. We can also say that "identity" is the sum total of all of the things mentioned in the above section on ***"self,"*** including our looks and expressions, that make us a "person."

In addition, our ego is often understood or recognized as a "fixed" identity (or multiple fixed identities). For example, I *am* Edward. I *am* a man. I *am* an African American man. This is *my* book. Jocelyn is *my* wife." These are statements made because I believe that I'm a physical body in a physical universe. My brain gives rise to these static thoughts, giving "me" consciousness.

POES

Primary Operating Ego Structures (POES) are identities like those mentioned above that we recognize and express as representing who we believe we are. These identities are formed through our own personal thoughts and perceptions. But, what we understand as "personal" mind is actually only one point of view within the greater or Collective Consciousness.

Collective Consciousness

There is really only one mind in existence appearing as many, and each of us can experience this Collective Consciousness by exploring what we perceive as our "own" mind.

The Collective Consciousness is the manifestation or expression of all thought form into physical experience. Physical experience consists of thought that has been given substance by feeling, and feelings are always founded upon one of two emotions: either fear or Love. Nevertheless, it is important to remember that fear is love turned inside out and upside down in the mind to create the illusion of separation. Therefore, everything in physical experience is given substance by Love. *In truth, Love is all that exists.*

We, as members of the human species, suffer consequences for believing the ego's story of separation. Some of the penalties we might feel are isolation, competition, or threats of loss and pain. This is why when it is disconnected from our Soul, the ego is perceived as the "bad guy." We take on an imagined identity as who we are, and then we relate to everything and everyone through this limited perspective. This prevents us from experiencing the depth and joy of our uniqueness, and obstructs us from the intimate relationships we crave.

Disowned Identities (DI)

As discussed in Chapter 4, *Disowned Identities* (DI) are those unconscious or suppressed identities often referred to as *shadows*. These personality traits or tendencies are disowned or abandoned by our *Primary Operating Ego Structures* (POES). Our POES want to control and protect us from risk and vulnerability. They want to manage and guard us from our real and imagined threats of pain and fear. When we cling to stories in our minds and call them TRUE, we also suffer in the shadowy regions of these *Disowned Identities*.

Although reprimanded every time they emerge, since we deem them as totally unacceptable, our Disowned Identities express themselves as emotional energy patterns and behaviors, often of a distinctly negative quality. Because they are dominated by our Primary Operating Ego Structures, DI can be overpowered, but never totally destroyed. Rejected energy patterns live on in our subconscious mind and arise once vulnerability is triggered. When they are discovered to be lurking within us, they ignite intense emotional reactions. For example, our Inner Critic and Wounded Child represent our ego's most profound and repressed DI. The more we try to restrain or reform these energetic expressions, the more depleted and diminished we feel, physically and emotionally, and the more likely we are to act out from that wounded perspective.

Inner Saboteur

Another one of the DI to be aware of is our *Inner Saboteur.* It is expressed as any behavior, thought, emotion or action that blocks us from getting what we consciously want. Our Saboteur is the inner conflict that exists between our conscious desires (e.g., "I want to find lasting love") and our unconscious dis-owned internal programming— ("I have got to be careful. People will take advantage of me . . . ")—that then manifests in self-sabotaging behaviors. Such a denied identity prevents us from accomplishing our dreams and reaching our goals. It does this by protecting us against life's disappointments and keeping us restrained and confined within our limited comfort zone.

Whenever I would undertake the new challenges, I felt compelled to pursue my Inner Saboteur was triggered, revealing its darker intentions. Like many entrepreneurs I would get charged up and passionate about a new endeavor, but once I began pursuing the goal I would inevitably become overwhelmed and begin to panic. My story was always the same. *"I can't do this without someone helping me."*

This self-sabotaging thought would compel me to begin searching for just the right "expert" to rescue me from my fear of failure. I was always convinced that experts were better equipped and smarter than I was, more proficient at doing the tasks I endeavored to pursue. Once I found and hired this supposed "savior," always at great expense or sacrifice, I would predictably discover a reason to be disappointed with them. I would conclude that this expert had "feet of clay" and did not know what the hell he was doing, and that I was wasting my time and money on him. This pattern of behavior always left me feeling angry, disillusioned and foolish, and it triggered my old childhood wound of feeling alone, disregarded and unsupported. I felt like the Little Red Hen, in search of help in feeding her family, who then, predictably, would have to do it all by herself.

Generally, this undermining pattern of looking to be rescued was how I coped with most difficult situations. I am now aware that to some degree I unconsciously believed I wasn't capable of accomplishing or finishing what I aspired to achieve. And looking back at my ambitions, I realize I suffered from self-sabotaging patterns when I felt challenged because I was unable to manage these sometimes-over-the-top emotions. Overreacting in hysteria to events, circumstances and people, hindered my progress, and at key times prevented me from reaching my goals.

At great expense to my tight budget, I once hired a real estate consultant to help me identify an appropriate property for one of my new Charter schools. In the beginning he and his staff spent four months with me, in which the only work products were my answers to his ridiculous questionnaire on property usage. He never showed me one potential location! If I had been in my own Soul Power as Self instead of believing the story of my Inner Saboteur, this so-called preliminary step would have been completed in less than thirty minutes; but as always, I trusted the so-called experts over my own good judgment.

Six months into this seemingly bogus process and ten thousand dollars later, I was so triggered by my feelings of impatience with what was, and his disregard of my feelings, that I finally realized that he had no real intention of helping me to find a location. It became painfully obvious then that I had inadvertently paid him to drag this procedure out as long as he could, and as a result, he and his staff had no concern for my time, expense or business objectives. Even though my Inner Saboteur strongly believed that I would not be successful without the help and guidance of a qualified expert, my POES had enough experience and wisdom to know that depending solely on experts can be an unhealthy issue for me.

I have since learned that when reacting to feelings of inadequacy, I need to stop searching for experts to take advantage of me when I am feeling most vulnerable. Subsequently as I became more aware, I developed the capacity to accurately pinpoint the thoughts, feelings and actions that led me down the path to self-sabotage. By becoming more aware of the root of my emotional triggers, I was more skillful in putting a stop to old destructive patterns of behavior and learned to make different, more peaceful choices. I won't say that, when vulnerable, I am no longer triggered by the voice of my Inner Saboteur, but I am now more alert to recognizing this voice is not who I am. When the thought "I need help" shows up, I am now more able to discern that I'm simply having another limiting belief, encouraged to the surface by my insistent Inner Saboteur, and as a result, I no longer have to be entrapped in, nor endure, such a thought.

Working with the Aware Ego Process (AEP)

The Aware Ego Process (AEP) allows us to identify, express, and then integrate *these unconscious or suppressed identities (DI) and POES.*

As an example of how POES and DI affected our lives and how we can become able to use the Aware Ego Process to shift focus to the heart and what really matters most to us, I worked with a client who believed that people who were less advantaged than she were victims who needed help. She was raised in the upper middle-class, never wanting for anything. She believed that her higher income status was wrong, something to be ashamed of. Although she was extremely talented and resourceful, she felt her privilege was unearned. She would often take on encumbering responsibilities for those she believed were not as fortunate as she. For example, lending money that was never repaid, or moving less fortunate people into her home and when they could not or did not support her household, she reinforced her belief that they needed her assistance and that she was helping them. In addition, she isolated herself from relationships she considered insensitive to the plight of the poor, judging them to be superficial and oblivious.

My client's underlying POES had convinced her that the world is separated into those who have, and those who have not, and that it was her personal responsibility to correct societal evils and cultural inequities that were, to her, blatantly unfair. By defining herself as a Communist and a social activist, her "POES" narrowed down her perspectives regarding the realities of the world's economic injustices. She protected and toughened this identity by rejecting materialism and judging wealth as shallow and pretentious.

Added to these limiting beliefs, my client also felt insecure and overwhelmed by life most of the time, even questioning her own capacity to take care of herself, let alone other people. While believing in her negative stories about her perceived incompetence, even while she was making an effort to help the less fortunate, she would feel taken advantage of, disregarded, or inadequate to meet their perceived demands. And these were the very souls who relied on her, that she was trying most to help. This circular reasoning created resistance and ultimately resentment.

Telling herself these unchallenged stories, while endlessly repeating false claims and painful insinuations without questioning them, supported her dismal feelings of inadequacy. In this loneliness and isolation, she suffered depression, and that inevitably created a breeding ground for her POES to exaggerate her *shadow* identity of unworthiness.

She needed a tool, a technique, with which to begin unraveling those painful stories, and the process of awareness through inquiry was the quickest and most compassionate way she could free herself from agonizing.

Through the practice of inquiry, she learned that judgments about herself and imagined limiting and automatic beliefs were the basis for her unique suffering. Over time, she became aware that holding on to these sad stories was the cause of her suffering. By disidentifying with the tales of "being wrong" or "not enough," and through the Aware Ego Process, she was able to remember her true nature. This allowed her to become free to accept her life as it was, with more reliance on Self. And as someone with conscious awareness, she could still express her passion to serve and support less advantaged people in the world, while not personalizing their stories of perceived injustice, or her own perceptions of herself as a "failure."

She was able to see that her Primary Operating Ego Structures placed value on generosity, selflessness, and sympathy for those in need. Through her practice of self-inquiry (see STS Core Practices in Part Two) she learned that having financial resources and access to opportunities in addition to her heart-felt deep empathy and compassion for those who were in need, could not be wrong!

Compassion, clarity, and understanding are powerful human emotions that can generate and support a healthy, even transformational, evolutionary shift for all humanity on our planet. Nonduality supports the conscious understanding that we are all ONE and that we are responsible for one another. Believing she was wrong for her prosperous social and financial status was just another delusion that was revealed to her in Awareness.

We suffer when we create a story about what is, what was, or what will be, and call it "TRUE." We especially suffer over our fears, which are negative ideas about the future; however any negative idea can cause suffering if we believe it to be TRUE.

I discovered that when I believed my thoughts,
I suffered, but that when I didn't believe them,
I didn't't suffer,
and that this is true for every human being.
Freedom is as simple as that.
I found that suffering is optional.[6]

~ Byron Katie

Authors Hal and Sidra Stone claim in their classic book *Embracing Our Selves* that awareness, and the ability to step back from any experience, thought, or behavior and simply become a witness to it, brings with it the gift of a more loving perspective. *Witnessing requires an ego that is constantly in the process of becoming more aware.*

Although these choices are generally made by our primary protector/controller ego identities, as the ego separates itself from differing *Disowned Identities*, it becomes more experienced with, aware of, and distanced from them. An ever-expanding combination of greater awareness and experience creates what I am labelling the Aware Ego Process. Giving voice and expression without judgment to all of our DI is our only antidote for happiness. Over time, the Aware Ego with its more enlightened perspective, begins to develop real choices about what actions (or inactions) it wishes to take, while no longer demanding that we behave out of unconscious, negative and often harmful pre-programming.

Just as my client could accept herself and reconcile her empathy for the underdogs with her own success, we can understand who we really are through the practice of Self-inquiry, which is discussed in Part Two. Using tools found there, and further on, in Part Three, where we discuss the Core Elements of STS, we discover a life that is Self-empowered and free.

CHAPTER 6

THE WOUNDED CHILD

Always the innocent are the first victims.
So it has been for ages past, so it is now.[7]

~ J. K. Rowling

Looking back on my life I see that, like all children, I was born innocent, trusting and good. However, as I was growing up, certain events and situations happened in a way that forced me to shut down or lash out to protect myself, and to think of myself as a victim. My reactions continuously caused me undue grief and torment through childhood, my teenage years, and well into adulthood.

Many of us are living our lives through the filters and outlook of our wounded inner children. Our childhood traumas not only color the way we see ourselves, but they often blemish the way we perceive our families, relationships, careers, and the world. Our minds tend to believe these distorted perspectives because our memories seem to prove them true.

Because our minds believe these memories to be TRUE, our thoughts continue to look for evidence to support the old stories that keep us locked in a habitual cycle of pain, dissatisfaction and mistrust. Consequently, we anticipate—and even create—the expected results. Remember that the mind's job is to prove to us what we already believe we know.

It is fair to say that in each of us, there is an innocent child who has suffered at times. As children we all had trials and challenges, discontent and difficulty during our younger years, and many of us experienced emotional, physical or mental trauma. Our minds try to forget those painful times to protect and defend ourselves against future suffering, and most commonly, we believe we can't bear to bring up or look at the suffering again, so we stuff our feelings and memories deep down in our subconscious minds. Many of us never dare to face this child, even for decades—some for a whole lifetime—for fear of "unnecessary" anguish or unresolved disappointments.

Ignoring this wounded child doesn't't mean she or he isn't there. The wounded child is always there, trying to get our attention, trying to express the pain and fear as a child would, by being demanding, overemotional, and at times, unrelenting, or acting out of resentment. The child says, *I'm here. You can't avoid me. I need you. You can't run away from me.*

To attempt to put a stop to our suffering we send the child away to a deep place inside, as far away as possible from our conscious life. But we inevitably learn that running away from our pain doesn't end our suffering. It only prolongs it.

When our wounded child asks for care, love, compassion, and nurturing, we generally do just the opposite. We judge the child's behavior harshly as immature and refuse to give him or her what he or she most needs. We "hide" from our inner children because we're afraid of being overwhelmed with grief or fear or anger. Some of us try to keep ourselves constantly entertained, distracted, intoxicated or anesthetized, all in an attempt to avoid experiencing the trauma all over again.

The behaviors of our inner wounded children often show up most when we feel vulnerable, dissatisfied, or when things are not going our way. These behaviors are often expressed as anger, resentment, aggression, jealousy, or insecurity, and inevitably, acting out only reverberates in our feelings of guilt, shame, or unworthiness.

The path I pursued to awakening made it impossible for me to ignore the compulsive stories of unworthiness from my childhood that constantly multiplied over the years, far into adulthood. I had to learn to nurture, and then when necessary, "re-parent" myself in order to regain my lost innocence. I came to see that my story was fairly universal: an early sense of self-worth, then a loss of innocence; followed by repeating patterns that arose in response to perceived criticism; lack of sufficient praise from family and my environment; the experience of isolation and the sense of not being "enough;" and then finally, an internalization of the *shadow-self*, which I embodied inside of myself as the wounded child.

CHAPTER 7

GOOD TIMES

When I reflect back on my early childhood, what stands out is how exciting it was for me to perform for my family and have their acknowledgment that I was talented. Since I was born in the late 1950s, by the time I started school in the 1960s, it was thrilling to watch all of the rhythm and blues, pop music, and dance shows that were popular on television, like American Bandstand and Soul Train. Everyone was eager to watch when the Beatles or Motown performers showed up on the Ed Sullivan Show on Sunday nights. I would watch these musical artists like they were gods!

Some of my happiest moments were when my mother would put dance music on the stereo, and my sister and my brothers and I would compete for my mother's attention by dancing the latest steps we saw from television. I was the second oldest after my sister, who was always the adored princess, but one thing I was better at than all of my siblings was dancing and singing. I remember performing the Boogaloo and singing Freda Pane's song "Band of Gold" for my mother, with all my heart and soul. My mother would cheer me on and brag to everyone how talented I was.

By the time I was eleven years old I had convinced other children on my block to join a club I had created called "The Green Leaf Club."

Our slogan was *The Green Leaf Club is the only club on the block.* We turned this slogan into our theme song. I remember being energized about coordinating a performance with the willing kids in my neighborhood, who liked following my lead. We sold tickets and wanted a sizable audience to attend our show. My primary objective was to put on a show in which we could entertain our families and friends, but in my heart, I most desired performing to showcase my own talent.

The night of our performance was perfect. I remember the weather was cool and the moon and stars shone bright that evening. My mother allowed us to use our backyard for our single performance. I had coordinated with the club members for both group dances and singing performances, but I set myself aside as the only solo star. The song I sang was a popular song at the time by Jewel Akens called *The Birds & The Bees*, and I sang it that night with joy and passion, feeling like the popular singer Tom Jones. I can still remember the applause I got for that performance. I was shining in the light of audience approval and the knowledge that I was talented.

Something genuinely great happened later that year that changed my life forever! The school I attended was well-known for producing a community-wide theatrical production of a Broadway musical every year. That year the show was going to be the musical *The King and I.* Everyone in the whole sixth grade, which included over 90 students, was trying out for different leading roles. As I thought about stepping up and asking to audition for any of the minor roles in the play, I watched as the usual suspects, or popular kids, tried out for the leads.

I could relate to and felt inspired by one of the songs from the play called, "Whistle a Happy Tune." The lyrics started with, *Whenever I feel afraid, I hold my head erect, and whistle a happy tune, so no one will suspect, I'm afraid . . .*

On the final day of tryouts I mustered up enough courage to ask for a chance in front of the entire school. I stepped up to the microphone and began my song. Because I was used to singing and performing for my family, I felt pretty confident in my abilities and overcame my shyness. There was a part of the song, *Make believe you're brave, and the trick will take you far. You may be as brave as you make believe you are.* All of a sudden, the students in the audience started whistling along with my performance at just the right spot! Once I finished everyone gave me a standing ovation. The teacher/director of the play announced to the entire school, "We have found our King."

Playing that role of the King of Siam meant a lot to me. It changed how I saw myself. It made me feel proud of being me. I then started yearning for positive attention from others. Although I desired adoration and attention, I still was unsure of how to obtain it.

My Story

By the time I got to seventh grade in 1969, my confidence in performing was overshadowed by my shyness and insecurity in being overweight, and I was underachieving in school, reading two grades lower than I should have been.

I had always believed that my life had some type of predestination. I felt I was special and that one day I would be recognized for my greatness. Growing up as the middle child in a middle-class black family on Chicago's south side in the 1960's, I realized that my siblings were all bright, with many diverse talents. My older sister, Dawn, was most impressive and always recognized for her beauty and academic rigor. My younger brother, Paul, was athletic, very charismatic and charming, while my baby brother, Jerald, was cute, adorable and creative.

As a child I never demonstrated any of these special qualities. I was heavier than the other children, shy, and academically challenged in a family that valued being a cut above the ordinary. Being "special" was a badge of honor in my family, but the only badge I wore was "strange boy." My parents respected high scholastic achievement—or having some other obvious talent or gift. It made my parents feel privileged to have children they could brag about, and I saw that in their eyes, I did not measure up. Consequently, I felt I wasn't much to brag about. I enjoyed art and listening to music but spent most of my time alone. My parents saw me as sensitive and maybe softer than a boy should be. They thought it was strange that I preferred to spend time alone or with girls. "Why can't you find friends to play with, like your brother Paul?" my mother often asked.

My mother was from the school of hard knocks. She didn't believe much in nurturing and compassion. She was quick to spank and remind me of what I lacked or that I wasn't good enough. My grandmother told me once that my mother's harsh parenting was because she loved me so much. It sure didn't feel loving to me at the time. My father didn't talk to me much, and when he did, he was also unsympathetic and intolerant. Other kids did not seem to like me much either. I was teased and picked on by other boys. I spent a lot of time planning my route home from school to avoid the neighborhood bullies who seemed to have it out for me.

In seventh grade I once had a playground fight with a girl from my class. Her name then was Marqetta Rodgers. Afterwards my seventh-grade teacher made a statement in front of all the students that it was interesting that the two most unpopular students in the class would fight each other. What I most remembered about that comment was that she considered me "the most unpopular in class." This designation of "unpopular" was a slap for me, as I hadn't considered before that it might be true.

My memory of this childhood playground brawl haunted my life. I don't recall what the fight was about, but I do remember that the brawl was encouraged by other students in the class, who seemed to enjoy feeding on conflict. They could engage my anger because they sensed I had a fear of being seen as a coward. "Man, don't take that from her!" That was called "boosting" a fight. I may not have wanted to fight her at first, but once they triggered me through boosting, there seemed to be no turning back. Although our teacher broke up the fight and no one was actually hurt, my pride was bruised. Once more, my self-esteem had been threatened by another outsider—a girl who was probably only trying to protect her own self-image.

Because this shameful moment troubled me so, long after I was an adult, I reached out to her much later on Facebook, to apologize for my childhood conduct. I saw that she was now a minister of a church with three sons. When we spoke, I expressed to her my regret over my behavior. With warmth and graciousness, she let me know that she remembered our skirmish, and that she was also grateful for the closure. We now stay in touch as Facebook friends.

As you can imagine my childhood was not filled with fun and lightheartedness. Most of my time growing up, what I remember is feeling misunderstood, threatened, and unworthy. I dreamed of being popular and loved, the kind of boy that people might look up to and admire. I believed that one day I would prove everyone wrong, that they would see that I was "enough." but at that time in my life there didn't seem to be much evidence of that being true.

I believed I was too fat to have athletic endurance and agility. As a remedy for this insufficiency, early on, from the time I was a young child, I adopted what I believed was a more important and obtainable role, that of the responsible one. I was always the one who could be counted on, never got into trouble, and made sure that my little brothers were safe and protected from harm's way.

The Wound

On Christmas Eve every year my father worked to make extra money. He would come home early Christmas morning tired and ready for bed. As a result, I was responsible for playing Santa and setting up Christmas, putting together and placing all the toys and gifts that were purchased for my brothers and sister under the tree. My parents told me where all the gifts were hidden in the house and I understood what needed to be done. I never had the delusion that there was a Santa Claus, like other kids had, and that was okay with me. I was actually good at this responsibility and felt honored to be given this role. Back then many toys needed to be assembled, and I was especially good at following instruction manuals, something my father had no patience for. I believed the Christmas Eve setup responsibility was always appreciated by my parents, and it was something I did with pride.

On the Christmas of my eleventh year, I remember being especially excited. I knew that money in my family was always tight, but I had already seen in advance all of the great gifts that my brothers and sister were getting for Christmas. I was confident that my gift was just as wonderful as those of my siblings. I didn't care what the gift was, just that it would be picked out by my parents, especially for me. After laying out all the presents under the tree I went to bed that Christmas night wondering what singular gift my parents had selected especially for me.

When I woke up Christmas morning, I was enthused to see my siblings' reaction to Santa's gifts. I was proud of how I had assembled the Barbie Townhouse for my sister and the train set for my brothers. I knew my parents were happy and appreciative of what I had done. My siblings expressed excitement for all of the great gifts that Santa had delivered that Christmas morning.

All of a sudden, I became aware that there was nothing under the tree for me. With growing apprehension, I asked my mother where my gift was. At first she looked over at my father, and then she looked back at me with an expression of confusion on her face. "Baby, we forgot your gift. I'm so sorry," she said.

I tried to be mature and understanding, but I felt crushed. How could they forget me? I was so hurt that I decided to just go back to bed that morning. Then I had a devastating but ultimately self-soothing realization. It became crystal clear to me that my parents didn't care enough to even remember me on Christmas! At that moment I vowed to always put myself first, and never to truly count on anyone for anything.

And so, at the age of eleven, on Christmas day, my wounded inner child was born along with the *shadow identity* that developed from this trauma. Those murky beliefs about myself may have protected the rest of my childhood to some extent, but inevitably they turned into negative behaviors that began the cycles that confirmed I couldn't' effectively cope with mature adult life situations. This Christmas story may appear to some to be a simple family glitch. A mistake made by overwhelmed parents that could have been easily forgotten and forgiven. But my sensitive and innocent spirit turned this incident into a defining moment of personal pain and trauma that would continue into my adulthood.

CHAPTER 8

THE GROWN-UP WOUNDED CHILD

My inability to feel cared for or even important to anyone gave birth to my "wounded child" perspective and I spent most of my life in fear of rejection or disappointment, caring for others, and not expecting them to care for me in return.

What happened to me that Christmas gave birth to a *shadow identity*, a darkness in my personality, which became an unconscious part of my thinking that arose whenever I felt vulnerable or threatened. Although this identify was formed in my innocence and adopted for my protection, it became an important personality trait for achieving many of my life successes. Because I believed I had to take care of myself first, I was determined to get my way and never to settle for less than I felt I deserved. That meant getting "my way" even beyond reason, or despite others' negative perceptions of me. I became extremely self-reliant, self-referring, but also self-protective, even when I may not have needed to be. This guarded nature often enabled me to make hard, unproductive decisions, while disregarding others' feelings, in protection and favor of my own.

But that dark side to this wounded perspective also made me unwilling to feel the fullness of my life. In my vulnerability I created what I believed were safety "boxes" with unreasonable walls to protect me from hurt and disappointment. These safety boxes were stories like, "never give anyone a second opportunity to disappoint you," or "they are only going to let you down if you count on them."

I developed these stories in order to defend and protect myself from feeling that I was not good enough, or in some way, had been judged as lacking. I wasn't willing to see how my low self-esteem kept me from being able to count on anyone, not even myself. I would sell myself short more times than I would admit, to keep safe from feeling let-down or disappointed.

This over-protection of my feelings existed both in my personal life and career. I loved and cared for my family, but I was never sure of their love for me. It was obvious to my wife and I that our daughters wanted us to respect their choices as adult women. In respecting their choices, I sometimes felt that they were not willing to consider how their choices might have affected us. I think that at times all parents feel this about their teenagers or young adults' demands, but as a result, I was sometimes hurt by what I considered to be their "unloving" behavior.

For example, once I was awarded a plaque from the City of Fort Lauderdale at a holiday dinner affair. This was a generous honor in recognition of my accomplishments in community service. I eagerly invited my daughters to attend the awards ceremony so they could see their father be recognized and appreciated by the broader community, but they both declined. I took it personally that they did not want to come. I felt unloved and unappreciated. Even though in my heart I knew that they loved me, I wanted them to be more demonstrative, and they weren't. They were just being themselves and acting their ages.

For some reason this rejection felt familiar and seemed to ignite that old wound. I was again that 11-year-old boy on that profound Christmas morning using similar coping strategies to defend myself from disappointment: *I can't count on anyone to care for me, so I have to care for myself.* Even though I believed I was now a mature and reasonable adult man, after 40 years, I quickly became that wounded boy again. I saw myself emotionally overreacting to this situation. My wounded child wanted to withdraw and be isolated from others and at times would even act punishing toward anyone who would hurt me.

My wife and children often couldn't understand my extreme behaviors, and neither could I. I wasn't able to verbally express why I was feeling so isolated and bruised. This was a cycle of pain and disappointment, then remoteness, and sometimes retribution, that always ended in my shame and guilt. After some time of licking my wounds I would realize that my daughters had nothing to do with what I was feeling, and just how badly I was behaving. In this regard my family has been among my greatest teachers, supporting my soul's journey to self-love.

I had achieved recognition and success in my career as an entrepreneur, but I had never believed that I was intelligent, talented or successful enough. I had reasoned that my gifts of tenacity, single-mindedness, and devotion to causes were the reasons I was successful, but even in those areas where it seemed as though I excelled through what I did, I still felt I was not *enough.*

During my business career I became a recognized pioneer in the Charter school management industry, launching the first middle/high schools in the state of Florida. I dreamed of creating a revolutionary school design that brought high-tech resources and premium access to minority students in poor underserved communities. I wanted broad-based community influence and access to financial institutions that would support these young people, affording my Charter schools with the same material resources and opportunities that were available to students in the wealthier communities. I made the commitment to bring fair and equitable educational resources to poor urban families. I was passionate about this cause and believed everyone should be.

My stories of unworthiness kept me striving for perfection, more achievement and secret validation, believing that if the world knew how unique and talented I was, I would then be truly "special." And, like most children, I had always wanted to be considered special, especially to my parents.

Although my intentions were altruistic, and my success at producing high performing students had been well recognized, I always struggled to obtain enough material resources to give my students the educational experience I felt they deserved. Even though Governor Jeb Bush commended me with citations and letters as the founder of one of the highest achieving Charter schools in the state, I still struggled with considerable failures in raising all the money and resources that were needed for the students to succeed. All I could see was that these failures were proof of my inadequacy as an advocate. Instead of accepting this as a boost to my self-esteem, I believed that my schools were overlooked and underappreciated. My perception of public education was that poor children and their families were seen as unworthy of the same care and resources that children in wealthier communities took for granted.

Now as a victim myself, I could relate to the plight of this poor community. Through this compassion, I personally took on the cause and fought for programs and services, but at the same time I lost sight of my dreams for pioneering education reform. My vision of inspiring a new model of self-empowerment for schools was overshadowed by my own feelings of lack. By falling into the abyss of the struggles I was confronted with on a daily basis, I made my personal story of unworthiness my business perspective.

I lived in a perpetual state of dissatisfaction and anxiety, never feeling supported, and more often feeling unprepared and incapable. Although I wanted my passion for the lives of children to be an inspiration to others, I often felt that I had missed the mark. As a developer of Charter schools that supported at-risk students, recognizable achievements and success stories seemed rare. Although most of the students were wonderful, many of them brought the traumas from their home life to school every day. The families of many of our students were unemployed, felons, drug addicts and even abusers. Often there were incidents requiring either Social Services or police intervention. I felt like I was spending too much of my time putting band-aids on stab wounds.

One day I was correcting a female ninth grader on her behavior. She was screaming profanities and vulgar language at the top of her lungs at another student. Outraged and insulted by her behavior, in my anger I expressed my disapproval and accused her of shameful and unladylike actions. I even asked her what her mother would think of her disgraceful behavior.

After I berated her with my judgmental tirade, she suddenly broke out in tears and bolted down the hallway. One of my teachers, having seen me scolding the girl approached me in a very gentle way to advise me that this girl had lost her mother the day before in a drug overdose. I was both devastated and embarrassed by my own behavior. All I ever wanted to do was hold the light of love for all my students, but here I was tearing children down in their vulnerable moments.

This incident showed me that I was now recycling the bullying and intolerance my parents, teachers, and fellow students had heaped on me—all that I had endured as a child. I saw the student by herself later that day and approached her to apologize for my insensitivity. I noticed the hurt and anger in her face as I walked toward her. At that moment it was obvious she was unwilling to accept my apology, so I grieved alone in shame and despair. I was not sure how to forgive myself for the abuse that I had inflicted on her and her innocence.

CHAPTER 9

OUT OF THE SHADOW INTO THE LIGHT

Moving On from a Broken Heart

By all outward impressions I was very blessed. I had demonstrated to all that I had a beautiful family and a successful business that the community valued, but I wasn't grateful for any of it. Everything in my life seemed either wrong or not enough, so I was always dissatisfied or disappointed because I couldn't feel the appreciation I did have from others. As long as I related to myself in this contentious way, there was no way I would ever be happy. I was living a miserable, often thorny existence, believing that no one could relate to my suffering. So I suffered in silence. My wife tried to be a support and a nurturer to me, but her kindness would trigger more shame in me. I would holler at her for some irrational point, making her wrong so that I could be right. But after my abusive tirades, I would either become self-righteous and aloof, or guilty and ashamed.

At times this cycle of dissatisfaction and anger sent me into a self-indulgent and emotional disconnect. Once I became so isolated, no one else mattered, not even my wife and children. I would get caught up in justifying my pain, but also in rationalizing my insensitive and abusive behaviors. Isolation gave me permission to shut my heart down, especially in regard to the people that I loved. I knew my wife felt vulnerable and concerned about me when I shut her out. She is extremely sensitive when people she loves feel pain, but in those moments I felt too caught up in my mental drama of victimhood to consider her feelings. This abusive stance was my default *shadow* behavior, one of my Disowned Identities when I felt vulnerable. It always seemed safer to go into one of my DI rather than to open up and admit to her that I was in pain, feeling shame and unprotected, as I had felt in my family of origin.

To keep from feeling the powerful emotion of unworthiness that was at the core of my isolation, I would indulge in distractions. Distractions would always make me feel better for a moment, but inevitably cycle me back to even greater feelings of lack and shame. Guilt and humiliation became fuel for addiction. These emotions led me deeper into addictive behaviors, reinforcing the belief that I was weak, defenseless and unlovable.

At one point I found myself coming home from work every day and drinking until I was either unconscious or barely conscious. My choice of alcohol was good vodka, not the cheap stuff, but top-shelf quality. At first I started adding a little vodka to my juice with dinner. That felt harmless since I believed this first drink helped me to unwind from the stress of a difficult day.

After a while I began having a second and third vodka with juice after dinner. It seemed that the one drink wasn't working well enough. Things progressed quickly with a need to get numb in the evening. I soon found myself sitting alone every night on my patio drunk and barely conscious. Since I rarely drank in front of my family, they were not aware of how intoxicated I had habitually become.

One evening I was so wasted and sick from alcohol that I fell to the ground. All I could do was lie down outside like a townie wino until I was able to stand again. Once upright and mobile again, I stumbled past my wife into our bedroom where I fell once more. Right then and there, lying on the floor two feet from my bed, I had a profound moment of recognition. I realized I was becoming that pitiful drunk guy you see on television, the one everyone scoffs at, often behind his back. I didn't want to tell my wife how I had become addicted to alcohol. It was just too shameful to reveal that to her.

While lying there on the floor, I also realized I really didn't like to drink. I only wanted to pass out so that I could rest my mind. I was drinking to distract myself from the hurt and suffering thoughts that had created my way of life.

By the time I turned fifty years old, my life had become so painful from anxiety that it had begun to take a toll on my mind and body. For the first time I felt that my business had grown too big for me: too many employees, too many problems and not enough resources to solve them. I felt physically, emotionally and spiritually bankrupt, hitting bottom, or as some say, I had entered that "Dark Night Of The Soul," that difficult invasion of God's astringent Grace that ultimately eventually opens us to new realms of spiritual experience.

I had always been a devoted student of meditation and had used my Transcendental Meditation (TM) practice to manage stress since I was in my twenties, but was not yet able to see meditation as a path to enlightenment. I was intrigued with expanding consciousness and finding a path to greater awareness. For all the books I read and workshops I attended, I still couldn't comprehend what enlightenment might have to do with me. It seemed so elusive, unattainable and difficult. Like many spiritual seekers I believed enlightenment was only available to special people—great masters, or those who had awakened after dramatic events, near death experiences, illnesses, or unbearable suffering. Though my life was painful, I didn't believe I had suffered enough to be that kind of special.

I am now aware of how my broken heart called forth this miracle, this Dark Night of the Soul, into my consciousness, but I certainly was not aware of it then. I was so consumed with my perspective of lack that I was not able to see that it wasn't "me" who was suffering. It was the addictive thinking or negative program, running itself through my ego or lower self—but I was not my thinking! My conscious mind understood the concept of addictive negative programming, but I had no idea how deeply this programming had infiltrated my subconscious mind and infested my thoughts, and just how deeply I was committed to my own suffering.

With the STS core practices I started to become aware of how unloving and judgmental I was toward myself. My personal self-talk was harsh and unrelenting. I wasn't willing to let myself off the hook for anything. And as a result of my unforgiving self-judgment and blame, I felt unworthy of success, undeserving of the praise and acknowledgment that come with it.

The Secret

I was a wounded middle-aged man who had engaged in too many self-empowerment workshops, and read too many self-help books that were unable to make me happy or transform my consciousness to better cope with my life. Like many seekers, in due course I stumbled on the movie "The Secret" by Rhonda Byrne.

The movie was a compelling story of the power of the Law of Attraction. Simply stated, that "law" is about the ability to attract whatever we put our full attention on into our lives. As a *New Thought* philosophy, it uses the power of the mind to demonstrate how our thoughts become reality, how all thoughts manifest as "things" eventually. By focusing on negativity, on doom and gloom, we remained under a dark cloud. However, if we were to focus on healthier thoughts and positive reinforcement for them, the Law of Attraction ensured that we would find a way to realize and achieve those goals.

Although the Law of Attraction is a commanding and compelling concept, most people fail at it, and I came to see that the LOA had failed me. The tools used in teaching the Law are visualizing, storyboarding, affirming one's control over objects by creating what's called a "vibrational match" to attract the object, and affirming one's desires which are then marketed as spiritual slot machines. But this teaching failed to address the influence of our own resistance, and how wanting something can keep us trapped in an unhappy cycle of desire, disappointment and lack.

Resistance usually is the result of subconscious fears and doubts. By subconscious I mean we barely realize they're there. Yet, they sit in the background and stop our desires from manifesting. They act as counter-intentions or saboteurs of our dreams. The more attention and energy we give them by resisting, the harder it is to manifest what we want.

I became aware that my own unresolved resistance was the cause of my unhappiness. My mind was packed with subconscious repetitious programming that was making my life miserable. I believed that the only way to be happy was to extract these negative beliefs from my subconscious mind, but first I would have to identify, name and *feel* these malignancies of thought. That is where things got confusing for me. I had been through extensive therapeutic counseling, exploring my denigrating stories, only to be continually returned to the same patterns of confusion and problematic thinking. My instincts kept telling me that there was a better way.

CHAPTER 10

THE INNER CHILD AND THE INNER CRITIC

From years of personal therapy and workshops on healing, I had discovered that the inner dialog with ourselves not only sets the tone for our emotional states but also establishes the quality of our life experiences. In addition, I learned that if I was committed to the radical healing of my wounded heart, a more responsive dialog with myself needed to be encouraged and expressed, with genuine willingness and determination on my part. To find this inner fortitude I knew I would need to begin having some honest conversations with those aspects of my personality that judge, demean, and tell me who I should be. You know which parts those are . . . They are the parts of me that would undermine my self-confidence and cause me to feel bad about myself. I knew in my heart that such a dialog would reveal the key to resolving my resistance and eliminating the negative patterns that denied me happiness.

The Voice of the Inner Critic

It is unclear when we start to hear any kind of conflicting inner dialog, but let's assume that the voices of internal programming begin when we first learn language, at around 12-18 months of age. During this time of development, we are also learning to walk and assert independence, so it makes sense that the voice of the Inner Critic begins as soon as we hear the word "NO." Feeling our parent's distress when we are headed toward danger or seeing their anger when we're doing something they dislike becomes an impetus for our inner conflict and subsequent remorse.

At this vulnerable and impressionable age, young children have not yet been socialized and are actually unaware of right and wrong. They are innocent and receptive, and their unblemished psyches are open and easily affected by criticism. The child has a compulsive and human need for belonging and acceptance by family and community for his or her own preservation.

Consequently, whatever the parent articulates, whether it is loving and encouraging or critical and angry, the child uses it to divide the world into "good" or "bad." As a result, the child develops both the positive voice that encourages and offers helpful commentary, and the Inner Critic voice that corrects or disciplines and provides mostly negative feedback. The more sensitive the soul, the more wounded the child becomes from negative correction, and the bigger the voice of the Inner Critic becomes. However, the more positively adults talk to the child, the more affirmative and loving the inner voice can be. Life always reflects back to us the love and nurturing we have received during our Innocence. By learning to cultivate a dialog between the Inner Child and the Inner Critic, those souls who were not encouraged and supported in their youth can foster a loving relationship with their blameless and pristine, innate self.

As an adult, my Inner Critic stayed busy keeping me on a razors' edge with anxiety and thoughts of unworthiness. I have since learned that like most people, my Inner Critic was largely the by-product of childhood authorities or power figures from my early innocent years.

During this influential stage of development, my Inner Critic adapted warnings and lessons from these powerful forces and internalized them. Their lessons encompassed ways for me to remain safe, to be productive, to act morally, and to be well-behaved. These powerful and prominent people included my parents, teachers, or any other authority figures that played a role in my care, by persistently pointing out to me what I was doing wrong. As a result of this scrutiny, by the time I reached adulthood my Inner Critic had adopted an abundance of judgments about me. My Critic was always prepared to embellish my perceived shortcomings with enough judgments to keep me oppressed, contained, and under control.

Although my Critic wanted me to be happy and successful just like my original loving, protective caregivers did, my conditioned Critic only saw me through a magnifying lens that showed my faults and rough edges. He was afraid and anxious, continually reminding me I was never going to amount to anything, saying . . . *That was a big mistake. What in the world were you thinking? You'll never get away with that! That's going to be too hard. You're just too lazy or, If only you were more attractive.* And my favorite story of all was, *I'm just not smart enough.* These are examples of that nasty manipulating voice my Inner Critic used to keep me in line every day. Determined to emphasize my insufficient and intolerable personality traits, my Critic was unyielding in its efforts to teach me to be a good, well behaved person. However, that was at the cost of my self-esteem and feelings of worthiness.

Establishing Boundaries for the Inner Critic

Kate Swoboda encourages us not to try to silence the Inner Critic. Her assertion is that it just doesn't work. On her website: "Your Courageous Life," she states, "If you put a muzzle on a streetwise dog, sure, it won't bite, until you take the muzzle off. Then you're *really* going to get it. If you want to stop a dog from biting, you need to rehabilitate it. You need to teach it a new way of being, not shut it down and hope for the best."

Taming or evolving our Inner Critic is accomplished when we first embrace our ego in present moment awareness, or awareness of Self. With Self-awareness we begin to realize the critic's voice is not "bad or wrong," but based on how it operates. *It's just an inner voice that has discovered how to respond to life in a particular way. It just* is*—and is part of all of us.*

If we're planning a journey to self-love and acceptance, then let that voyage start with accepting that the Inner Critic is *there* and will always be there. By using the STS tools in this book, we can also know that, with greater awareness, our Inner Critic's voice can be managed and even significantly changed over time. By acceptance, I'm not saying to let the Inner Critic voice run wild, displaying inappropriate behavior toward us whenever it wants! But we can stop imagining that suppressing or disowning our

Critic's voice is what can fix the problem. Only acceptance and creating new *boundaries* for our Inner Critic, can appease its disapproving nature.

Taking a Breath

Establishing boundaries for our Inner Critic is achieved in the same way we would establish them with another person. Like all relationships, but especially the relationship with self, we should begin a practice of engaging each contentious interaction with ourselves by requiring that the communication be considerate and respectful. The moment our Critic says something judgmental, condescending, blaming, or shaming, we need to respond by first *taking a breath.*

A momentary breath gives us a spacious moment of awareness, in which we can respond to our Inner Critic with earnest statements, like "I will listen to your fear and distress, but they must be voiced respectfully" or "I understand you may be feeling exposed and defenseless right now, but there is no need to personally assault me. There really is NOTHING WRONG WITH ME."

Initially, talking to ourselves in this way feels odd or a little strange, but what we're actually doing is reprogramming an old fear pattern or story. We're establishing a courageous habit of noticing the voice of our Inner Critic. Based on greater awareness, this empowering new habit supports creating protective boundaries when responding to our Inner Critic. This new practice will help us to both pacify and defuse the harsh judgements and condemnations that our Inner Critic often spews at us. Our Inner Critic needs consistent and vigilant boundaries to function in our best interests, so embracing this responsive relationship will monitor and cultivate our Soul.

If the Inner Critic begins to rage against us, we can use this practice of getting present with our breath and recognizing that our Inner Critic is engaged or overstimulated, instead of trying not to see or feel or hear it. Then we can begin to set boundaries with our Inner Critic in a way that keeps it from terrifying us with self-doubt.

Dialoguing with Our Inner Child

Because my Inner Critic had severely scrutinized me for most of my life, I became used to its aggressive voice and was passive to the disheartening internal program that incessantly played on and on in my psyche. I generally accepted the notion that somehow all of what it said was TRUE.

But once I began to realize that my Inner Critic's voice was in truth coming from an internalized, fearful and wounded child, it became important to engage my Aware Ego in starting a new dialog with the Inner Child who was still unblemished inside of me.

The Inner Child is our original Innocence residing deep inside of us and is a direct descendant of the child we once were. It is central to *SoulTranSync*™ practices to understand that the Inner Child is with us at all times, and may show up in a bigger way, unexpectedly, after certain desires and actions are triggered. Like the Inner Critic, our Inner Child is impetuous and spontaneous, often expressing him or herself suddenly, without us being aware of its presence.

My wounded inner child developed the false belief that Love was conditional. Instead of encouraging me to know that I was lovable simply for who I was, the Inner Critic bullied me with a limiting premise that I was only lovable and acceptable for what I did, or didn't do. My Inner Critic kept me believing that I was inherently unworthy and unacceptable even as a mature man. As I became more aware, I welcomed a fresh dialog with this part of me to affirm my true identity as Self and began nurturing my Inner Child. I am now aware that *the most important relationship that exists in the world is our relationship with our Inner Child.* To me it's the only one that matters.

One Example

As a mature and responsible man I pushed hard, sacrificing personal time and devoting serious attention to my career, never taking a day off and working most weekends. So an internal response through the eyes of my Inner Child might have been something like this: "While I put in numerous hours above and beyond the call of duty, why did my co-worker, who never made it to work on time, and left work early most days, get the promotion that I wanted? What about me?"

In such a situation, my Inner Child not only felt overlooked, but also disregarded. A reaction to such a disappointment would then trigger my Inner Critic, who might tell me I'm a sucker and I let my management take advantage of me. Then I would begin to question both my capabilities and self-worth.

Usually, I'd get lost in stories of career and personal failure, and then shut down from disappointment. But once I established appropriate boundaries with my Inner Critic *using STS,* I invited my Inner Child to be heard, and I was able to let the Aware Ego Process assist me in evolving. As a result of cultivating this discipline, I was able to take ownership of my wounded identities and recognize their presence within me. I can now allow their emotional energies to be expressed and felt, without clinging to judgments and illusions of being wrong and inadequate.

Nurturing Our Inner Child : An Exercise

If you can find a photo from your childhood, I would suggest that you put it on your phone or by your bed and regard it frequently. This will create a devotional image in your mind, providing encouragement and guidance for your Inner Child. It will also prepare him or her for the journey of the Aware Ego Process by expressing love and compassion.

Start by acknowledging your Inner Child's wounds and feelings, and ask him/her for permission to begin a dialog. Ask what you can do to help your Child feel better supported and cared for. Promise to always be available by keeping a dialog between the two of you ongoing. Affirm that you'll never abandon him or her again. Your Wounded Inner Child may at first appear tentative and afraid of this different form of attention. But over time, your Inner Child will start to become more confident as he/she evolves through Soul Awareness.

If sincerely nurtured and attended to, your Child will be able to realize that he or she is safe with you, and that there is only the unblemished innocent Inner Child within. Our Inner Child becomes capable of helping us navigate the vulnerable moments in life, and becomes a supportive partner.

Healing the Inner Child

It shouldn't surprise us that the Inner Critic is negative about, and unsupportive of creating a new relationship with our Inner Child. The Critic believes that this more confident partner's voice is not real, might be dangerous, and ultimately is not worth our time.

Through the SoulTranSync process, using an Aware Ego perspective, the condemnation of our Critic can be overcome. This is a significant first step in any serious Inner Child healing. To know ourselves from a Soul Awareness angle, we have to clear our hidden agendas by resolving our Inner Child conflicts. We do so by letting go of fearful stories, releasing imprints from trauma, and eliminating negative programming that has created confusion in us, distractions and dramas, all of which have tended to monopolize our attention.

If you are interested in furthering your practice of Inner Child nurturing, and quieting the Inner Critic's harsh voice, I suggest you read the book *Homecoming* by John Bradshaw. It's a profound tool for growing a strong bond between you and your Inner Child for the purpose of healing. Also, you can purchase a meditation on nurturing the Inner Child at my website www.soultransync.com.

PART TWO

THE SOULTRANSYNC PROCESS

THREE CORE PRACTICES

EMOTIONAL SELF-AWARENESS

Introduction to Part Two

Part One of this book was written to provide a context for Soul Transcendence and to introduce us to the Three Core Practices of SoulTranSync (STS), which transformed my life very quickly from powerlessness to self-empowerment and happiness. In Book 1 I revealed my personal stories and deep childhood wounds and discussed how trauma to my innocence created a veiled perception of reality, which haunted me throughout my adulthood.

To review, the Three Core Practices, as stated in Part One, "How to Use this Book", are already known to you:

1. **Non-duality or Oneness:** The awareness of non-separation or oneness with all that exists and the discovery that separation is illusory (Discussed in Part One).
2. **Self Inquiry:** The contemplative tool that when used can tame the mind to point us toward SELF, and the Awareness of the truth of our nature. This will be discussed further in Part Two.
3. **Ho'oponopono:** The devotional self-identification and forgiveness practice that uses the mantra: "I love you. I'm sorry. Please forgive me. Thank you." This will also be discussed further in Part Three.

In addition we have defined the Soul in this way: Soul is the spiritual part of a person or self, that is believed to give life to the body, and in many religions is believed to be eternal.

Introduction to Core Practices

The practice of SoulTranSync is made clear and relevant by first introducing us to the core components of the practice. These well-recognized and effective teachings of Self-awareness are Non-Duality, Self-Inquiry and Ho'oponopono. For the very first time, STS introduces and incorporates these three transformative approaches to Self-awareness into one seamless practice.

- ***Non-Duality***, the knowledge of non-separation or oneness with all that exists, enables *us* to discover and accept the true nature of awareness. In Part One we explore the philosophical understanding that we are all individual manifestations of *one* universal energy (or SELF) and that we are connected in powerful ways.

- **Self-Inquiry** is an ***Advaita Vedanta*** practice that encourages us to participate in an internal dialog in which we question or inquire about our true nature. In Part Two we discuss the process for uncovering our essence in any circumstance and we come to realize that we are not this physical expression, but an aspect of an eternal unchanging SELF with more potential than we can imagine.
- **Ho'oponopono**, the ancient Hawaiian practice designed to "make things right," allows us to clean and clear any thoughts, perceptions or beliefs that may limit us. In Part Three, we learn the Ho'oponopono mantra and its impact on aligning us with our true nature, enabling us to discover and fully embrace our Soul Power.

These three teachings worked together to *elicit* major transformative chang*es* in my outlook, *revealing* a profound understanding of my "true nature." It *is* my greatest intention that as you progress through the three parts of the book, *you will* Uncover and Embrace your own Soul Power, *as I have.*

But the first requirement is that you, the reader, realize that you are not who you think you are. Having the willingness to open your mind to a totally contrary image of yourself is the starting point to Soul Transcendence, or Self-realization. Any practice or teaching of Self-realization has to push our comfortable boundaries and challenge us to question the truth about our genuine identity.

Throughout this book there are STS exercises to help us with Soul Transcendence. Relating to ourselves through introspection and contemplation can be a little disconcerting at first, but with practice our attention to the outer world is shifted to the Self, where an innovative dialogue can begin. This conversation with our "self" then directly enables us to move toward a replacement narrative of positive self-identity, one that supports, nurtures and cares for our greater good.

Before I became committed to self-realization, I was compelled to defend my beliefs and stories as both true and real. This meant defining or identifying myself with stories about who I believed I was. These identities were often tricky and always self-defeating. Because I was stuck in this powerful subconscious programming, I continually sold myself short.

One story that I would habitually suffer in was that I was not as smart as I should be. I believed that in order to be what my mind thought of as ideal, I needed to be smarter. I was always in a perpetual search for what I believed was "smart," giving what I believed was smart more credit than it deserved, while at the same time deprecating my own intelligence. This awkward tale I told myself had me always looking for the expert who could rescue me from my limited abilities. But as with any false God, I inevitably became disappointed or disillusioned by my rescuer, triggering another limited belief that no one could be counted on to care for me.

This vicious cycle of limited thinking left me feeling unappreciated, unsupported, and hurt. Even though from all the outer impressions, I was living an abundantly blessed life, I never felt happy, contented or peaceful within.

Such perpetual thinking became the landscape of my life, and as a result of these stories, my body and mind took on incessant pressure and pain. You may have heard the term, "the issues are in the tissues." This statement means that whatever resistance you hold onto long enough, will take up residence in your body and your cells, and cause you pain and/or disease.

STS practices are about releasing resistance while cleansing and purifying your Consciousness. As spacious awareness permeates our bodies and minds, a new vibrational alignment lifts us out of pain and suffering into peace, self-love and self-acceptance.

In these pages, we learn about Self-discovery, and elevating our vibrational alignment. As we read and absorb each chapter, we start to experience profound shifts in our beliefs. We begin to see our lives as more expansive and aware, and let go of defiant or challenging issues that cause us suffering. And, we feel our *"self"* opening up to the love of "*SELF*" through the presence of our Soul-*Self,* enabling transformation in our lives, as disabling and patterned thinking shifts. We sense these changes being made all the way down into the core of our being, our innermost hearts.

Deborah King, author of *Be Your Own Shaman* wrote that it is in the heart that we can come into universal love and dissolve the illusion of separateness. That is where we can heal, she believes, emotionally and physically. It is when we open our hearts to love that we can both forgive and connect more intimately with ourselves and others, rise above lower emotions of anger, hatred, and envy, and ascend to a higher state of consciousness. "It is in the heart center that you experience peace and deep inner balance,"[9] she states.

As we move through each chapter, we experience energetic shifts in our consciousness. Please give yourself permission to read chapters over again as needed, so that your heart may gradually gain awareness of this fresh state of being, and can release the stale and uninspiring thoughts of your mind.

The immediate and palpable result of this kind of heart awareness, is what I have called “Soul Transcendence.” This means once the heart has begun, to open the Soul begins evolving, which is sensing oneself rising above limiting situations and seeing them instead as challenges that create newer and more aware perspectives. At this point, we don’t have to solve anything! Our attitudes and behaviors automatically shift as we attune and align with Self, that capacity within us that reflects our highest values, or that has Soul Awareness. With practice, we automatically resolve what were once considered thorny problems.

Soul **Awareness** is a positive state of being. Once established in Soul **Awareness**, we are no longer bound or influenced by lower vibrational levels like shame and guilt. We are living with purpose and driven by inspiration. Soul Transcendence is the natural outcome of Soul Awareness and it becomes our default response to any resistance or dis-ease in our thinking.

The STS exercises in this book are meant to lift us into higher, subtler, refined states of awareness and perception, prompting us to break through the illusions created by living in this world, to open our hearts, and to bring us into a greater, more conscious, awareness of the Soul.

I suggest you adopt some of these exercises as daily practices. Exercises can be practiced within minutes and done anywhere, but they are all very simple and life transforming. When we begin this process of Self inquiry, our questions become more open ended and non-judgmental; e.g., I can ask myself the larger question, "Who am I?" instead of believing in something imprisoning that is simply not "TRUE."

To summarize, we discussed three definitions of the word self in Part One: "self" as the "me" with a body and all the attributes of being here, in this relative, material world, limited, dualistic, and ever-changing, what most psychologist refer to as "ego"; Self as a conscious Awareness of the "me" or the Aware Self that allows all thought, feeling, sensation and perception to appear just as is, without choice or preference. The Aware Self acts as a link to a vaster non-manifest realm; and to SELF, as that realm, the all-pervading, omniscient field, of the ONE, and what some refer to as God.

CHAPTER 11

THREE CORE PRACTICES

My path to Self-Awareness required examining what I sensed were the essential practices for spiritual alignment, and the STS Core Practices were adapted as a set of guidelines that would most inspire soul revelation. A Soul revelation is the sudden awareness gained through a striking disclosure of truth. Revelations often involve direct insights into something that had never before been realized.

These practices offer clear, researched and tested teachings that encourage this kind of revelation. Each one of these practices has been exercised for centuries. Taken together, these practices multiply the effectiveness of having such "epiphanies" and have far-reaching consequences for personal growth and Soul Transcendence. Therefore all of these practices are geared toward relating to ourselves with fresh and unique perspectives, in order to learn who we are as Self. Unless we are willing to explore the truth of who we are, we can easily remain trapped in the illusory nature of the mind.

Because of my addiction to the story of unworthiness, I knew I needed to start with questioning all of my beliefs, not just the ones that made me feel bad, but also beliefs that I counted on to define myself. Was I a good person? Was I a reliable person? Was I a loving person, or was I just a self-centered narcissist? I became aware that identifications I had with roles and behaviors had the potential to become a trap for suffering. I knew that to free myself from these traps I would need to challenge all of my sacred cows.

For example, I believed that I was a loyal friend who would be there whenever I was needed. When examining that story I saw that my relationships were often of a codependent nature, and that my need to identify myself as loyal had a Shadow side. This side could cause me to feel unsupported, or disappointed, if I judged that someone was not as loyal as I was. Sometimes I felt people took advantage of me. I learned that the family and friends I felt were so loyal were only human, and that human behavior was flawed, and that they often could not be counted on. While I felt love and affection for them, I had to realize that I was not responsible for them or their life situations.

I have learned that loyalty should first be to our Selves. Learning to be loyal to my Self is a continual commitment that is explored every day in every relationship I have, but such a commitment must begin with my own self-worth.

Self-worth became the impetus for my quest for spiritual alignment. If I was going to love myself and believe that I was deserving of love from others, I needed to begin inquiring, "Who is unworthy?" or "Who believes he is unworthy?" Was unworthiness the truth of who I really was, and if I thought so, how was I so sure it was true? TRUE means that it can be proven. Could I prove that I was unworthy? If I couldn't prove that to myself, then maybe it wasn't true. Then who or what was I? This was how I began my Self Inquiry.

The American Institute of Vedic Studies, made up of teachers of ancient Indian scriptures, calls Self-Inquiry an introspection process or meditative form, which involves tracing the root of thought to its origin in the heart.

David Frawley, the author of *Vedantic Meditation: Lighting the flame of Awareness* wrote, "the practice of inquiry requires understanding ourselves on all levels of body, mind and spirit, particularly the deepest level of heart".[10] Heart awareness is about accepting and respecting our own feelings, no matter how painful and deceptively inappropriate they may feel. Learning and accepting our own vulnerability, and becoming the holder of our own heart means taking responsibility for our own feelings and choosing not to be a victim by opening the space for better self-understanding and self-forgiveness.

Non-Duality: The First Core STS Practice

"Go to the pure I AM. Not I am this or I am that, but simply I AM. Then throw out the I, so that there is only AM. This is the stateless state, the ultimate principle, the absolute Self. Everything, in essence, is this absolute principle called the Self."[11]

~ Adyashanti

The first principal practice for STS is the awareness of Oneness, or what we call Non-duality. Non-dual Awareness is essential to spiritual alignment. It is the awareness that only GOD exists, and that everything else is one's own perception. Non-duality discards all ideas of separation from anything and anyone. In that Oneness even we are a fundamental aspect of all that is, and the illusion of separation is a psychological deception. We are part of and made of one Non-dual Consciousness. From our human perspective, our lives can be seen as something akin to what the Hindu traditions call "Maya" or illusion, like a dream state, and we may wonder why we don't experience our life in this extraordinary way.

Things can appear different, or not the same, without being separate. Just look at a simple flower like a daisy. The petals are a little different from each other, but they are not separate because they all are part of the flower and arise from the same stem. Similarly humans, plants, and all the objects of the world are different in their appearance and functioning, but all come from the same Source. This one Source of intelligence, what some call "God," is behind all life, and has an infinite number of expressions that we acknowledge as unique from one another. But all objects, including our identity, are only as real as our perception of them.

We live in what appears to be an abstract universe created by the mind. The mind "holds" aspects of intelligence, including consciousness, perception, thinking, judgment, and memory. It encompasses both human reasoning and thoughts.

The belief that "I am a separate individual" is the "dream" or "illusion" that is the cause of all psychological suffering. Our illusion as a separate self is held in place by the mind, and its deep-seated habitual patterns, which maintain the illusion.

The mind also creates the concepts of past and future, which don't exist. There is only ever Now.

Non-duality has nothing to do with trying to become more loving. There is, however, a tendency with greater awareness to become more loving and open. Openness and love are just side effects that appear to happen when the illusion of a separation is penetrated.

Non-duality is about what is true, not what you want to be true. You may want to be more loving but non-duality is about what already is right now.

Similar to the desire to become more loving, the pursuit of happiness can be elusive. The perpetual drive for happiness is actually a form of suffering. But when there is no "self-entity," the neurotic drive for happiness naturally dissolves, revealing the arising of joy.

One of the practical applications of Non-duality is demonstrated in how we develop empathy and deep understanding for one another on a human level. If we become aware of every human being as our own Self, perfect, whole, and complete, we no longer have to experience feeling threatened or fearful of one another.

Self-Inquiry: The Second Core STS Practice

The second principal practice of STS is the contemplative tool of Self-Inquiry, which can lead one directly into a non-dual perspective. Inquiry uses and can 'tame' the mind to point us to the universal SELF, and the Awareness of the truth of our nature. This practice has the ability to pull us out of identification with the constructs of our minds and remind us of the larger picture, as Self, which mediates between SELF and our ego nature, self. Part 2 of this book will offer a fuller explanation of this practice.

As my stories of unworthiness began to unravel, so did my mind's habitual engagement with these disempowering, un-self-loving stories. The simple techniques of Self-Inquiry and Non-Duality are two of the most effective practices we can use for Self-Awareness.

But I also became aware that spiritual alignment can be supported and accelerated with a devotional practice of clearing stressful memories, cultivated through forgiveness, and nurtured in acceptance of our innocence and one's wounded inner child.

Ho'oponopono: The Third Core STS Practice

The third and final core practice of STS is a powerful ancient Hawaiian devotional practice that includes a mantra, called Ho'oponopono. Ho'oponopono is a healing practice that works through "cleaning" or "clearing".

Many people have understood Ho'oponopono to be a mantra where one repeats the words "I love you, I'm sorry, please forgive me, thank you", as a form of mental and spiritual cleansing that could be equated to Buddhist or Hindu techniques for purifying negative karma. However Ho'oponopono is defined as a forgiveness and reconciliation practice, removing errors of thought. This practice presupposes that error of thought is the origin of all problems and sickness in the physical world.

The practice also teaches us that we are in some way responsible for everything that appears in our life simply because it *arises in our life*. Like non-duality, it teaches that there is nothing else in life except You, and that if we encounter resistance, violence or anger in others, there must be something in us that mirrors these same tendencies.

By adapting this non-dual perspective, I now see that the external world and the inner world of thoughts, memories and feelings are not separate; instead, they are seamlessly one. And because this world arises within me, I can do the cleansing needed from and for the collective mind.

Universally across most cultures and religions, it is understood that the concepts of “thank you, I’m sorry, please forgive me and I love you” are all valuable and important. So consequently, the power of Ho’oponopono may come from the sheer volume of people throughout human history who have agreed that these concepts are valuable, important and useful to humanity. It’s a rare thing for the vast majority of humanity to be in accord about anything. For this reason I believe Ho’oponopono expresses a level of awareness that extends far beyond its Hawaiian roots, and perhaps has relevance for every culture that has ever existed on Planet Earth.

Through the practice I have become aware that by chanting these nurturing words, I am tuned into the frequency of the words and the intention they carry, even if my inner resistance to reality is sometimes triggered. I have found that these four simple phrases act like tuning forks. Each phrase is carrying a different tone of purity that I can use to synchronize with my Soul and my Self. With this inner alignment, I refresh my mind. By applying this chant to the chaos of my mind and those conflicted parts of myself, stillness and calm result instead. Part Three of this book is devoted entirely to the practice of Ho’oponopono.

Non-Duality, Self-Inquiry, and Ho’oponopono are the three primary Self-realization practices of SoulTranSync.

As soon as I began to comprehend then implement this trio of disciplines into my spiritual practice, I experienced a profound awareness and a clarity with the realignment of my thinking. These SoulTranSync practices have transported me to the brink of enlightenment, since I undertook to commit myself to them. In them I have found a simple, fast, and effective way to live in peaceful inspiration, and my life has never been the same since.

CHAPTER 12

AWARENESS AS AN OUTCOME OF SELF-INQUIRY

The simple practice of Self-Inquiry is our best tool for expanding our awareness and enlightening our minds. First, we use our emotional reactivity to a negative situation or a conviction about something to examine our stressful beliefs. Then we put the harmful belief into the form of an inquiry. This two-part practice is best performed using an intense emotional trigger; however, it can be just as effective with our everyday anxiety or stressful thoughts.

For example, when people arrived late to a scheduled meeting with me, I felt disregarded and disrespected. Feeling disregarded is a triggered emotional response that arose during my anguished childhood. When I felt disregarded by someone I would sometimes respond with anger, or with detachment and intolerance, or at times with a combination of energies resembling passive-aggressive behavior. The disapproving behaviors I demonstrated, either ignoring or punishing those people, often produced guilt and shame feelings inside me. To suppress those feelings, I began to justify my behaviors: "They deserved the way I spoke to them" or, "I can't put up with their crap." I interpreted the disrespect very personally as an assault on "me."

Inquiry cuts through all the drama by directing our attention away from the person (that "me") who appeared assaulted and attunes us through our Selves, to our true SELF instead. By using inquiry to reflect on different perceptions of our selves, we discover shifts are available that can take our attention beyond whatever the suffering is that we are experiencing in the moment. We are consciously challenging our relationship to the "sufferer," while no longer affirming it as who we are. If we are willing to realize that the SELF is vast and undivided, we cannot identify our self as separate, inadequate and incomplete. Immediately, who we really are takes that particular *"you"* off the hook._We can see that "you"—or—"I" is free, and therefore, can be relieved of the idea of being a victim of someone else.

How Inquiry Works

Here's an example. No matter what emotion you find yourself entangled in, take a moment to thoroughly feel it. Take a deep breath, then exhale, allowing your attention to be on feeling the emotion. How intense, dull, or painful is it? As you feel the emotion, begin to observe your thinking, and see how quickly your emotions start identifying with stories.

Now, begin your Self-Inquiry, avoiding further entanglement with a sense of the identity of a "me." Ask yourself: Who is the "I" that is sad? Who is the "I" that is angry? Who is the "I" that is afraid? Who is the "I" that is offended? Who is the "I" that is overwhelmed? Who is the "I" that believes it's not good enough? Is that the true "me"?

As you investigate the source of your "I-thought," find out where it points. To whom does it refer? Look behind your thoughts. Look underneath your emotions. From where does the voice of "I" originate? You will soon become aware that it is the idea of "me" that feels this emotion you're experiencing, not the true you. It is an identity we created for ourselves that feels this way.

We are attached to many memories, opinions, beliefs, assumptions, and expectations. Without awareness, the tales we tell ourselves arise from, and can chafe at a wound, or aggravate that victim identity until it is raw and festering.

It is important to remember that the "I-thought" is merely a character created by our imagination; it identifies itself with whatever the mind and body perceives. This "I-thought" is the birthplace of all misperceptions.

For instance, if "I" am disappointed because a situation or circumstance didn't go as I'd planned, or I believe someone has betrayed me, then the "me" who is disappointed is really the hopeful thought that things "should" have worked out in "my" favor. But then the "me" discovers that it didn't!

By assuming we are that "I-thought," that "me" is who I am, the mind becomes attached to the story of "me" and begins to feel distress. In other words, it is the "I-thought" that is hurting—*not the Self.* This distressed imagined self *identifies with* its feelings. "This sadness is mine!" it exclaims. But emotions cannot be owned, only experienced, just like any other phenomena . . . including our thoughts.

An Example of Inquiry

Richard is a friend of mine, who sometimes feels intense loneliness. His loneliness can be triggered by something as simple as not making plans with anyone for the weekend. Our fear of being alone is one of the mind's great challenges. Fear of isolation, or being left out, is embedded in our human psyche. An unplanned solitary weekend stirs up feelings of sadness, of being abandoned and friendless. With these emotions Richard begins imagining other people warmly sharing experiences together, having adventures, or making love, while he is all alone. Richard confesses that some weekends he sits at home with the blinds closed, thinking about all the things that have gone wrong in his life. When the mind is left to its own devices with an emotional problem, it seeks out evidence to prove what it believes. It does not matter if it is true or not, the mind wants to be right.

Richard is also an aware being. He understands that when he doesn't question his stressful beliefs he suffers. We all get caught up in delusions sometimes. This is human. Once Richard remembers inquiry he begins to question the identity of the "I" that is lonely. He tells me that the moment he begins challenging the "I-thought" with the question, "Who is aware?" his mind becomes spacious again, and he is able to let go of the thinking that is caus ing him to suffer. He answers with "I am," acknowledging the deeper truth of his nature. He believes that this simple practice has changed his life. Letting go of the identification with "the lonely guy," has opened his mind enough to be able to enjoy his weekend solitude. He also sees that he is never alone when he has himself. He is whole, present and unbroken.

The Embodied Aware Self

Inquiry returns us back to an Aware Self, which is our embodied consciousness that connects us to our Source, or SELF, and reveals to us our true nature. We can no longer be the collection of memories and thoughts we have believed our selves to be. Now we are in the presence of an inner awareness that perceives them. Our Aware Self is liberated from the beliefs about our selves that we hold; it can withstand our "I-thoughts," because we see through the emotions we might be having at any given time. Our Aware Self only experiences these perceptions; as the liaison to the SELF, we see that we are the Subject perceiving life, not the Object perceived.

If we accept that reality is non-dual, then it follows that conscious awareness has no parts, and that only the SELF exists. That Subject or SELF creates objects; without the Subject there are no objects. The "objects" are only apparent in the relative world, not actually anything separate from Awareness itself. While the appearance of objects creates the illusion of duality, actually it is only "apparently" dual. In truth, we are all one with everything.

What is important to understand is that our freedom is based on the self's relationship to the perceived objects in our lives. Since the SELF creates everything, it is not attached to anything. We are free when we are aware that we are the embodied Self, merging as Awareness with apparent objects... released from the burden of desiring objects, but aware of the gifts of their beauty and diversity.

Like the analogy of clay becoming the pot, the object we call a "pot" is made of clay and fired to be a pot, which then becomes an object, but the clay as the subject can be molded and take on multiple forms (i.e., tools, bowls, art, and even a home to live in).

Our minds believe in suffering as though it is an object, just like the pot. But in another moment, with inquiry, mind may be able to witness that suffering is not some "thing," not an "object" at all. With this awareness, suffering can be collapsed back into Awareness itself, through shifting our attention to kindness for ourselves, or even by focusing on some other object. Once we get into neutral and out of our judgments, our suffering has many alternatives.

No thought, judgment or perception that we can imagine about our selves can ever truly *be* or *define* our Aware Self. It is beyond any concept our mind might try to convince us it is. Our Aware Self is the Presence upon which all experience is made conscious. We experience emotions, but we are not them. Emotions are energy in motion, only showing up as revealed in Awareness. Who I am cannot *be* guilty—I can only *experience* the feelings of guilt. Who I am cannot *be* wrong—I am *experiencing* the ego's emotional challenge by identifying with being "right." It is significant to realize that like all objects, our emotions are impermanent and will change. Negative thoughts that we anxiously beat ourselves up over are temporary too, and *shall pass*.

In author Michael Singer's book *The Untethered Soul*, he writes that "There is nothing more important to true growth than realizing that you are not the voice of the mind—you are the one who hears it."[12]

As we begin to practice this form of Self-Inquiry, detaching from that voice in our heads, a safe-haven arises, where the seat of our

Soul lies. This is a precious space that we can always return to for an aware perspective, allowing our "me" identity to lessen, recede into nothingness, that spaciousness from where it came.

With a committed practice of inquiry, we begin to feel that this spaciousness is who we are, our identity, our home. When we start living a more self-actualized existence, one in which our relationship to the objective or causal world is critically altered, we begin to reside in the love and bliss of the Self.

The Questions of Inquiry:

"Who Am I? Who Is Aware? Am I Aware? Am I That? and What Am I?"

These questions of Self-inquiry divert attention and curiosity inward toward the truth of our true and original nature. By focusing attention away from outward objects, events, and experiences, we allow ourselves to experience our inner world. Frequent inward focus leads to an experience even beyond experiencing itself, a dimension that is empty of any experience or sense of self, with deep realizations that are beyond description.

Self-inquiry enables us to use any question that directs our attention to our sense of "me" or toward our direct experience of our existence in the moment. For example, if I find my attention directed to an outer sensation or experience, like the frustration of battling heavy traffic, then I can ask, "To whom is this sensation of frustration happening?" The apparent answer is that it is happening to "me," but with the practice of inquiry we don't stop there. We ask again, "Who or what is this "me" that feels frustrated?" By repeating these questions new experiences of "me" arise, taking the experience and the experiencer deeper into inner "knowing" of our being. There are no wrong answers in Self-Inquiry; anything we experience or observe about our selves is part of the truth of the moment. Therefore, a discovery of "Who am I?" is possible . . . and can definitely appear through such Self-Inquiry.

Once we are aware of this discovery, a surrendering to the truth of who we are becomes foreseeable in us, as it penetrates our consciousness. All of our inner energies that were previously activated by thoughts, desires, and our personality are now released into peaceful, spacious Awareness. In fact, this spaciousness is the quality of everything that is eternal, and anywhere we find our Self, as mediator between the ego self and SELF, there will always be this same sense of space.

Continued and committed practice of inquiry inspires peace, joy, love and compassion in us, all of which lie just beneath our constantly assessing, shallow nature. And when uncovering a profound truth about our nature, we can proceed to inquire further: e.g., "If I am even more than infinite peace, then who or what am I?"

Inquiry may also reveal that everything that exists holds some consciousness, and therefore we, as conscious beings, can tap into this unity consciousness as if we are One with everything, as One Being. Awareness, emptiness, spaciousness and oneness are all fundamental qualities of Being. When Self-Inquiry exposes an essential quality of our existence, that's another layer of "Who am I?" to be discovered. Then we can ask beyond even that. As another example, "If I am more than pure awareness, who or what am I?"

As the process of exploring identity through inquiry unfolds, we may want to try more creativity with our questions. One inquiry question may be more effective for us for exploring that spacious Awareness than another inquiry might be.

What is valuable to understand, is that this practice of Self-Inquiry is guiding Awareness or attention to parts of our own experience: the parts that have not been consciously realized yet. Initially this means directing attention inward to more subtle aspects of our individual experience. As we reach more universal dimensions of Being we notice that it no longer matters in what direction our inquiry is directed. All roads lead to SELF, through Self.

The following is a list of inquiry questions, or approaches to inquiry, that can assist us in expanding our awareness. Answering these questions is a form of mindfulness meditation, pointing attention away from the body/mind construct or identity, and deliberately pointing us toward Self-discovery. This new "identity" is one that is greater than the limited identities of the mind and can be cultivated through our inquiry. The whole becomes greater than the sum of its parts.

Who am I?

When asking ourselves the question, **Who am I?** our thinking immediately starts exploring the limitations of a separate self. We soon become aware that any restriction from our "POES" becomes synonymous with the reason why we suffer. By responding to this question with the answer, **I am Conscious Awareness** our minds begin to relax, releasing the hold of a particular identity of a separate self. A beautiful feeling of Presence expands and deepens as we begin recognizing and aligning with the Self. The question **Who am I?** repeated with sincerity, as often as possible, will support this feeling of Presence.

Once we acknowledge ourselves as Presence itself, our identity starts to get comfortable in its true nature, and the mind, personality, thoughts, and beliefs begin to recede in importance. They are still there as tinctures, tinting our consciousness and hinting at what is fading away because they have been seen through and are not given as much of our focus as previously. This alone reduces the notion of suffering, as we can directly see the effect of conscious Awareness on who we otherwise believe we are. More often, as we permit ourselves to rest with this Presence in Awareness of the present moment, we stop getting caught in the past or the future, which actually cease to exist. This happens in the NOW, instead. What a marvelous feedback loop for ourselves! And by becoming aware of this sacred NOW moment, our bodies, minds, personalities, thoughts and feelings can align in harmony and freedom, instead of perpetual suffering.

As discussed in Part One of this book, conscious Awareness is the ability to experience or to feel wakefulness, having a sense of Selfhood, or possessing a Soul. In other words, conscious Awareness is the state or quality of being aware of an external object, or something within oneself.

Who is Aware?

With the inquiry question **Who is aware?** we begin declaring Conscious Awareness by answering, **I Am**: "I am the one who is aware." Through this declarative, "I Am," we allow ourselves to feel an unbounded limitless spaciousness. "I Am" signifies that there is a "sense of existence" or there is "knowledge that I exist." "I AM" is synonymous with Consciousness and includes the sense of being alive, of being present. "I Am" is the love of Being that is the source and cause of all desires and our creative impulses.

This inquiry answer "I Am" leads us to the profound question of "Where is this 'I" that is aware?" When we realize that we cannot find an entity called "me" that "owns" or possesses awareness, we begin to realize that maybe we are the Awareness itself. This recognition cannot be understood by the mind. It's a leap that the mind can't make, because awareness of itself is an awareness of **facts** about itself: "I'm a man, I'm a husband." Mind cannot sense that which is beyond the mind, where there is no "me."

Am I aware?

The inquiry question "Am I aware?" asks us to remember our true nature as Awareness. Remembering to *recognize and align with* our aware nature is the fundamental intent of Self-*Inquiry. The question,* ***Am I aware?*** prompts a direct answer in the NOW moment of "Yes, I am aware." This answer is only relevant in present moment awareness. Once thought and relationship to time are involved, there is a perception or an identification with a "somebody." The vastness of Awareness includes everything but is not specific to a 'body. "We are that Awareness too.

Am I that?

The inquiry question "**Am I that?**" can be particularly helpful when we become aware of our mind being pulled into an illusion by our emotions. I feel intense sadness, so the illusion is: something has got to be wrong. Or I feel a sense of insecurity, so the illusion is: I must be insufficient or inadequate. When our emotions are raging, inquiry into the truth of any limited story can be a direct path back to Self. By answering this question with a **No, that can't be who I Am,"** we give ourselves an immediate sense of spaciousness. This happens because the truth of who you are as an Aware Embodied Self ultimately can't be anything except conscious Awareness.

Am I . . . ?

Am I a nice person? Am I smart enough? Am I on the right track? Am I in love? Asking questions such as these invites a debunking of the myths of our minds by exposing them to the light of Awareness. An inquiry question beginning with **Am I?** challenges our programmed knowledge of our imperfect self. This knowledge can either define the limits of our recognized identity or point us to a greater Self that has no fixed identity and is neutral, or, we can say, toward a more perfect self-reflection, as Self. Neutral does not mean we are without passion for life, nor does it mean we don't care about people or unjust circumstances. It only refers to the judgments that we cling to that are not in our best or most loving interest.

As an example, if I ask the question of myself, "Am I smart enough?" and I avoid simple answers, like "yes," or "no," which are judgments, I can dig deeper. I can ask, "What is *enough?"* which can even be measured to some empirical satisfaction. Also, I can ask, "What is *not enough?"* Can that thought, *not enough* be considered with intelligence, without some qualification or reference? Not enough for what? And as well, what defines *smart?* What are its criteria and/or limitations? And then last, is *smart* something that *I* am?

With this inquiry, the answer to **Am I?** may end with **I don't know what I am or I don't know who I am**, which are both useful answers to the question.

Once we recognize and accept the answer **I don't know,** we begin to feel the open spaciousness of this neutrality. What might that space feel like? Experience that feeling in the body, right down into the cells. What is there? What might have been just an abstract thought in the mind, like nothingness, or emptiness, has been converted into something that is visceral and kinesthetic. Not knowing allows for possibilities and expansiveness. Notice what neutral feels like; what discovery about ourselves does it reveal? By narrowing the question down to **Am I?** we could be open to other possibilities of inquiry. For example, **Am I?** brings the questioning down to something existential; the simple fact of whether or not we exist. In fact, this question might also be expressed as **Do I exist?**

The question **Am I?** points to the simple fact that we ***are***, in spite of what we are experiencing. Underneath everything that's going on, there is a sensation of existing. This inquiry question also points to a dimension other than experience.

When that sense of existing is in the seat or center of awareness, it's possible to explore what's true about one's existence. Imagine what it's like right now to just be. In this Now moment is it enough to just exist? If we've been told all our lives that it's not enough to be who we are, that we should be smarter, richer, more attractive, more enlightened, more compassionate, more loving—or what have you—then how would we respond to this sensation—at last—of being *enough?*

I used to believe that if I could just *be* what I was **supposed** to be, I could then accept myself. For instance, let's consider the illusion of being wealthier. Like many men, I believed that being richer or smarter would be the external confirmation of having or being *enough*, and that would translate to being whom I was supposed to be. But how much is *enough* and how can that be measured?

It was meaningful for me to use the inquiry question **Am I?** to discover both the extent to which my existence was enough, and the extent to which I thought it wasn't. **Am I wealthy enough?** was the question. The first answer that arose in response, was **I don't know.** I was conscious of all the empirical evidence that pointed to my belief of financial lack, but in meditation I began to explore the feelings of not knowing. I soon realized that in the Awareness of not knowing was a spaciousness, even a peaceful resolve. All judgments of my thoughts of insufficiency began to feel illusory and insubstantial. The *I* that believed this erroneous thought was *me*, and *me* was only a phantom. I didn't have to bother with *me*!

When we decline all identification of who we believe we are as not our "I," what remains is something that cannot be described, only lived. This gives rise to an impersonal "I Am," which is not the object of thought, because it is above and beyond thoughts and the mind. It is indescribable, although we may try very hard to describe it. You can know, experience, and be this "I," but you cannot think about it or analyze it, as it is not an outside object. **This I Am consciousness is the real you.**

It is relevant to understand that questions of inquiry would ideally be answered in meditation. Contemplative inquiry will not be soul-transcending if it elicits answers that are merely rational and intellectual. Inquiry that is not heart-centered can stimulate the mind and make the process of inquiring nothing more than a mental exercise. Once we give up the struggle to "know" the answer, we can arrive at a state of complete and open attention.

By open attention I mean not preoccupied with achieving one thing or another. It is-impersonal attention, free of attachments, judgments and labeling and is often referred to as "witnessing consciousness." The witness, as subject, does not lose itself in the knowing of the object, but maintains an awareness of the heart, the source of the attention itself. **In open attention** we stay in the present moment perceiving any sensation or impression that arises in the body, while retaining an impersonal posture of witnessing consciousness. This position is then full of love and free of the need to analyze, label or conceptualize.

In open attention our perceptions become transparent and even illuminating, since **there are no more thoughts to label that which**

is perceived. We now relate to any experience in an intimate way, without prejudices or expectations.

This heart-felt state of open attention is only possible if our ego—with its personality, memories, stories, illusions and judgments—does not intervene. Therefore, *one* should ask the essential question, "***Who am I?***" without expecting a rational answer. Rather, asked in a state of curiosity, we can then surrender to the possibility of a mystical intuition about who we really are.

CHAPTER 13

DEVELOPING EMOTIONAL SELF–AWARENESS (ESA)

Self-Talk

The voices in our heads are incessantly speaking to us, often repeating the same things over and over. For example, "You are spending too much money" or "You don't need to eat all this!" Many of these thoughts are triggered from our childhood distress, when we were teased and made to feel ashamed, or hurt because we did not have the material things we felt we needed. We also learned to think these habitual thoughts from experiences with our primary caregivers as we grew up, and we have been repeating them our whole lives. Considering the fact that cognitive abilities do not fully develop until the mid-20s, we can imagine how staggering the number of these thoughts that no longer serve us might be!

As a child I was called husky, the code name for being fat or larger than most boys. This was not only embarrassing, but shameful. Even my mother teased me. Although I was thin by the time I was 16 years old, the imprint of childhood obesity stayed with me throughout adulthood. The thought of being overweight even now can cause me to feel stress. However, as a result of Emotional Self-Awareness (ESA) I am able to relate to that thought differently. I no longer believe the emotions that are triggering my feelings of vulnerability are wrong.

As we discussed earlier in the book, to become free and fully realized in the Self, we will have to accept and love all the parts of us, including choosing to be vulnerable sometimes.

But few people consciously choose vulnerability. The stakes seem to be too high. Most of us feel that if we reveal our *Shadow* persona we *expose ourselves to being named, shamed and blamed . . .* misunderstood, or worst of all, rejected. The fear of rejection from others can drown us in a sea of unworthiness and *humiliation.* "They are going to see that I don't know what I'm talking about" or "They are not going to like me if they know that I feel insecure."

Our Inner Dialogue and Dissonance

For us to grow, it is imperative we develop awareness of our unloving inner dialogue. The ability to choose how we think about ourselves allows us to regulate our responses to any emotionally triggering event. Starting now to become aware of what we tell ourselves inside, in any situation, will help us choose responses from Awareness, rather than from emotional reactions. Our sense of autonomy and clarity depend upon it.

If we understand that our thoughts activate emotionally weighty, often painful, processes within us, we can master the way we encounter them. Our thoughts, and the underlying beliefs that drive them, unconsciously trigger negative emotions, but we do not have to react to the "effect" of them if we are aware that we ourselves are putting the judgment on them.

For example, due to socialization, programming, and identification with our society's collective moral ethics, my beliefs about justice and fair play are aligned with most self-identified moral and ethical people. So, when a perceived intruder unapologetically steps over me in front of a line, an old pattern of judging others and righteous indignation are triggered in my mind. My sub-personality "Inner Critic" immediately begins judging her character as unprincipled, self-centered and egotistical. I start to believe that I have become a victim of her bad behavior. Emotional energies begin showing up, and most of them feel uncomfortable or full of anger or hurt. These emerge because I believe that I have been disregarded, or disrespected, as I was in childhood, and then embarrassment shows up for not standing up for myself and insisting that this woman go to the end of the line. In victim mentality, I have very few thoughts to explore and all of them are negative. When I do not judge I have a multitude of thoughts about the situation I can explore, and, potentially, I can choose to believe or not believe that I am a victim.

Although some of these negative or victim beliefs fall harder on my psyche than others, I become riveted on what I consider her unscrupulous behavior and in the collection of negative stories I run in my so-called mind, I see her as a brazen line jumper! So I then begin assessing her ethnicity and even gender and feelings of entitlement, as my primary points of reference for these judgments. I think, "These white women believe that they don't have to submit to standing in line. They are not aware of anyone else in line who matters, so they feel unconstrained and believe they have blanket permission to get in front of everyone else, and that's not fair." Having misogynistic and racist thoughts like these ignites an even lower vibration of energy of shame and guilt in me. This is because *I* want to believe that I'm not prejudiced or racist *or sexist,* and I hold a strong resistance to racism and intolerance of any kind. This inner conflict causes me to struggle with *dissonance,* believing that my values of racial and gender tolerance are in opposition to what I was—in all honesty—feeling and thinking, just a moment ago. Although I am annoyed by the perceived social slap or assault on my integrity, it is this ***dissonance*** that is the cause of my suffering.

Every time I attempt to shift my attention to a more aware and peaceful outlook, *(This is not personal, it's only a perceived assault, because there is nobody being hurt here.)* my thinking remains fixed on the injustice, specifically on the race and gender of this brash gatecrasher. The longer I'm in line with this blatantly unapologetic woman, the deeper I dwell in judgment and intolerance of her behavior. And now I have added a new layer to the suffering—a strong belief that it is wrong to think like this: *(I shouldn't feel this way, it's wrong to judge anyone in this unfair way.)* This is falling victim to the "effect" of our thoughts . . . when we become aware that we are passing judgment on an "other," and therefore, on ourselves, simultaneously.

Although events and other people's actions may prompt unpleasant feelings and reactions, they do not cause them. The real triggering agents are what *we* tell oursel*ves.* Most of our interpretations of the present moment are operating from the subconscious or unconscious mind. They *store* all of our previous life experiences, our beliefs, our memories, all the situations we've *ever* been in and all images we've ever seen.

It is important to remember that long-term suffering like unhappiness isn't exclusively induced by thoughts or emotions, for these always come and go. But agonizing and prolonged unhappiness happens when we repeatedly cling to conclusions and the judgment of those thoughts and emotions, e.g., *I don't want to feel this way; it's wrong.* Once we believe that we are WRONG our minds will conjure up evidence to prove it so.

Another example is, *I have a problem controlling my hunger, so I eat too much. I am wrong (or bad) for eating too much.* The mind now has an ardent mission to prove me right in my self-judgment by citing evidence regarding my lack of discipline or willpower in my eating choices. These unsupportive thoughts make eating distressing and then mock my self-esteem. The judgments we have about ourselves keep us caught in a futile cycle of wanting something different than what is and then reject who and what we actually are. This cycle of dissatisfaction has an energetic vibration that continues to promote more discontent, until we paint our entire life as insufficient, lacking in the ways we believe "matter."

Understanding Emotional Self-Awareness

Emotional Self-Awareness (ESA) is most powerful when we can accept reality as it is. In the above example, "reality" becomes the thought and emotional trigger that "I eat too much." Accepting this thought doesn't make it true, nor does it make me wrong. But judging this thought as wrong—for example, I *don't want to have an eating disorder*—can foster an underlying belief in myself as a weakling, without sufficient will, but this cannot be true as Self. This thought is only reflected, or mirrored back to me through the collective mind, which is also who I am.

ESA is a practice of remembering that our thoughts and emotional energies are never anything to worry about or refute, but we do need to be aware of them. Only with Awareness can we begin transcending our raw resistance, easing our suffering, with more self-acceptance and compassion for ourselves.

Developing Emotional Self-Awareness is the first step toward transforming our thoughts and feelings. Our **Aware Self** wants *to be aware of what we think and how we behave, to shape the quality of the events in our lives and their effect on our hearts.*

Emotions and/or Stress

Through Awareness our emotions can become useful as compassionate guidance systems, instead of unwitting traps for misunderstanding our life circumstances.

Feelings, by themselves, do not create problems.
It is rather the tendency to interpret and analyze them.
When out of habit you believe those interpretations,
it is there that the suffering begins.[13]

~ Mooji

In the sea of life, feelings are our navigation system. Like a compass, our feelings indicate when we are on or off track in relation to where we want to be. We all have goals, or a vision of what we most desire and want to see happen in our lives. Success in overcoming problems and navigating challenges is directly related to our ability to experience a full range of emotions, allowing them to inform our decisions and keep us in touch with reality.

Pleasant emotions such as joy, confidence and happiness, tell us that we are getting some of our inner goals met, but these feelings can be misleading. Not all things that create happy feelings are healthy or in our best interest. "Feel-good" addictions like food, drugs, or even sex, can produce a range of emotional consequences, from mild to devastating.

Stress in any form can also be damaging. By definition, stressors are life events that are capable of creating negative effects in our physical, mental, and emotional bodies. Life's disappointments, like losing a job, financial challenges, illnesses, car accidents, or other mishaps, can generate resistance and excessive pressure on our minds, our hearts, and our bodies. These stressors can be positive in moving us toward changing something that needs to change in our lives, or they can be detrimental, causing us to feel vulnerable. They can also affect our bodies adversely. Stressors force us to adapt to new conditions.

Eustress

Eustress, a term coined by endocrinologist Hans Selye, is taken from the Greek prefix **eu**- meaning "good", and the word **stress**. Eustress literally means "good stress." This translates to a form of stress from which one can benefit, as in increased job performance, or in taking on new challenges that we enjoy. It can ignite our passion for what we are engaged in and enhance our general well-being. It's a positive reaction to stress that generates a desire to achieve and to overcome limitations, such as fears of change and challenges to the status quo.

It is important that we experience eustress. Without it, we may become depressed or feel a lack of meaning in life. Eustress motivates and energizes us to work on a difficult task, which, in turn, can offer huge satisfaction. For example, some people get excitement from scuba diving and would experience eustress while engaged in the activity; while on the other hand, those who are afraid of water could find even the thought of scuba diving effects them negatively.

Eustress can arouse our courage, resilience and fortitude, and at times can motivate a better response to, and perception of, what causes us stress in the first place. To boot, Eustress enhances our creativity and resourcefulness because we are responding positively to stressful situations. It shifts our perceptions from the constraints of reason, from what we originally perceived as possible, and takes us outside the box of our own limitations. Those who experience eustress are flexible enough to note that the perception of insurmountable obstacles that appear in one's path on the way to where we are going, can—and do—shift to surmountable challenges instead. As a result, we can develop a positive point of view toward challenges, instead of a dire or frightful one.

Some events that cause stress, like dealing with important goals or accomplishing great feats, are healthy emotionally, mentally and physically. To do extraordinary things we often have to push beyond our comfort level. This resulting stress helps us to learn, grow, perform, excel and create greatness. However, it is still stress and as such can create wear and tear on the physical body. If we learn how to take breaks, or relax, for example, with meditation or yoga or sports that develop our chi, or we allow ourselves quiet or down time to savor the sunset, one another, or our pets, we create fresh neural pathways to promote inner peace. By letting go of the do-er from time to time, we can enjoy what it is we are striving for, as it unfolds, moment by moment.

Our emotions give meaning to life and connect us to other people. They help us to understand ourselves and how we relate to others. We can think clearly and creatively when we are more aware of our emotions. Emotional Self Awareness helps us manage stress and better navigate through life's inevitable challenges. ESA also encourages effective communication with others by displaying trust, empathy, and confidence. Without ESA we can unknowingly spin into confusion and negativity.

Emotions are a constant presence in our lives, influencing everything we do. ESA assists us in getting in touch with what we are feeling and why we are feeling that way. With ESA we learn how to identify and express what we are feeling from moment to moment, and to understand the connection between our feelings and our actions, no small thing. ESA also helps us understand what others are feeling and gives rise to empathy for others.

Facing Stress Using Emotional Self-Awareness

Any painful, unpleasant or "feel bad" emotions such as anger, guilt, shame, hurt and anxiety are essential to ESA. They provide significant information to us that pleasant emotions can't. They enlighten us about where we are in relation to where we want, aspire or yearn to be, but they are NOT an indicator of what's wrong now. This is the greatest and most common misunderstanding of how we interpret our emotions. They are only an invitation to understand what possible actions, or changes, would better support our vision or goals. Challenging emotions could even be calling us to replace limiting beliefs with life-energizing beliefs.

I have always admired people who appear comfortable in their own skin, and when speaking publicly are warm, humorous, confident and compelling. But I was terrified by the thought of speaking publicly. I would shake and sweat and sometimes feel like I would black out. Once I got to the podium my confidence was nonexistent. I was so emotionally wrung out that I believed my performance was an embarrassment. I soon started avoiding the risk of having to speak in public, or if absolutely required, I would over-prepare by writing down every word I needed to say and then reading aloud rather than just speaking naturally. I believed that I was incapable of speaking extemporaneously. Because of this overwhelming emotional trauma, I was certain that public speaking would never be a part of my future.

But ESA allowed me to re-examine this dream of mine. I began to see that my intense desire to be good, if not perfect at public speaking, mixed with my underlying subconscious feeling of unworthiness, had created a perfect storm for my imagined problem. Once I took my attention off of how horrible I felt preparing and performing publicly, I began finding ways to make the experience playful and fun. I turned the stress into *eustress*.

I also became aware that I had created an ideal public speaker in my mind that didn't appear to be me. This confident, articulate speaker was always ready to stand in front of anyone, at any time, and impressively connect with an audience. By examining this belief, I came to realize that I had not only created an "ideal me" to compare myself to, but I was judging myself against an "ideal me" that didn't even exist. This imagined identity was the problem, not me.

I now look at any opportunity to speak publicly as a gift. Sharing my thoughts, feelings and experiences in front of a group can still be a little scary, but the reward of touching others' hearts and inspiring my audience is worth facing the fear. Fear is nothing more than a thought anyway!

Emotional Self-Awareness is a skill at which we can become proficient and, with patience and practice, can be mastered. The practices found in Chapter 13 will help to develop our ESA by teaching us how to become more mindful of difficult emotions, and how to manage our uncomfortable feelings.

CHAPTER 14

EMOTIONAL SELF-AWARENESS (ESA) PRACTICES

A Breath Meditation Practice

The sensation of open spaciousness is the only true objective of this meditation, described below as the Breath Meditation. When the mind slows down and gets quiet, the body relaxes, and the in-breath and the outbreath flow effortlessly.

This breath practice supports our consciousness for ESA and strengthens our present moment awareness, pointing to the truth of our innate nature as conscious Awareness. This meditation can be an opening or a gateway into Emotional Self-Awareness, but can also be performed as daily devotion on its own.

The Breath Meditation

The following is an 8-Step simple breath meditation technique that is both easy to follow and effective to support mindfulness and the practice of non-attachment.

- Sit with eyes softly closed and turn your attention to the inhale and exhale of your breathing.

- Without attempting to control your breath, breathe naturally and slowly, preferably through the nostrils.
- Inhaling and exhaling to the count of 4 or 5 may be comfortable, but don't try to regulate or manage the breath.
- Become aware of the sensation of the breath as it enters and leaves the nostrils. On the inhale feel the cool air as it slowly enters your body, and then on the exhale, feel the warmed air as it leaves your body.
- As you exhale notice your body releasing and relaxing into itself. Concentrate on it to the exclusion of everything else.
- Although quite naturally your mind will be tempted to cling to different thoughts as they arise, gently release thoughts by remembering to return to the breath, and the sensation of release.
- If you become aware that your mind has wandered and is now following thoughts, simply return it to the breath and step 5 of this meditation.

Repeat these steps as many times as necessary until the mind settles on the breath. I suggest starting with five minutes and adding an additional minute on every practice. With a daily ten-minute practice of non-attachment, you can easily begin to create spacious awareness and a dis-identification with your thinking mind.

With **ESA,** uniting with your breath is a powerful method for becoming present or mindful, so master the above Breath Meditation first. By concentrating on each aspect of the breathing process, we let go of the past and future and are focused on the moment inside the breath. Conscious breathing sends impulses to areas in the brain that impact emotional reaction by relaxing and balancing our mood and supporting **ESA**.

The Emotional Self-Awareness Practice

After getting comfortable with the Breath Meditation above, and the mind is quiet, you can use this seven-step practice to develop Emotional Self Awareness (ESA) of your feelings and their connection to your thoughts. This simple exercise marks the beginning of mastering your emotions. To master an emotional state does not have to be difficult or distressing work, but it does require the willingness for us to feel our emotions. As we discussed earlier our emotions are energy. Allowing them to be fully expressed can transmute them into a higher vibration. To successfully express emotion we must first feel our emotional energy. This is done by identifying the sensations in our bodies, and then releasing their pull on our attention.

Focusing our attention on this energy can be the most powerful practice for transcending lower vibrational emotions like sadness, anxiety and fear. If we plunge our Awareness into our bodily sensations, Awareness reveals to us what is going on emotionally beneath the surface. Allowing ourselves to fully feel the waves of these emotional energies in our bodies will eventually diminish their intensity and sting.

It is important that this process is undertaken like a mindfulness practice and that we take the time to get it right. To succeed at freeing our self from emotional traps, stretching beyond our comfort zone is recommended, but please do not get overwhelmed in the process. This should be a gentle and loving process, not a form of punishment. With this mindfulness practice, we can immediately gain the benefits of relief in both our mind and body.

To maximize the effectiveness of the ESA Practice, I suggest we keep a response journal about our experiences. We remember not to activate our minds and learn to stay in our hearts while we use this practice. ESA practice is a cathartic exercise that can produce miraculous, life-altering results if we are able to trust it, knowing that in the resulting spaciousness, the truth of our tender hearts will be revealed. By illuminating the emotional energy or resistance we hold toward *change*, the resulting awareness of our habitual patterns will eventually ease us toward a more fulfilling spiritual alignment with who we truly are. Alignment means feeling good, and adhering to positive, self-affirming values, such as acceptance, gratitude and self-love.

Steps to Emotional Self-Awareness (ESA) Practice

Following are the steps to ESA. It's important that you give yourself at least 10-15 minutes to perform this meditation exercise. Refrain from pushing yourself if this becomes too emotionally intense. I suggest sitting in an upright or seated position, but what is more important is allowing yourself to feel comfortable and relaxed.

Step 1. Inventory your intense emotional states and identify their triggers.

Distressful emotional intensity is often revealed to us when we are in judgment or resistance to the present moment. If your trigger event is paying bills the first of every month, your stressful belief may be that you spend too much and are going to run out of money.

Step 2. Use Inquiry to ID the trigger and the causal belief.

Using the Self-inquiry practice in the beginning of Chapter 11, be aware that you are not your thoughts, feelings or emotions. And as the observer of your emotions, take a moment to become consciously aware that these emotions are most often from old and defiant fields of energy, like suffering in childhood, that may be unresolved. These old wounds have resulted in habitual patterns of behavior and reactions.

Now, as an intelligent and mindful adult, become aware of these processes at play inside of you and apply inquiry questions to the identified triggers. For example, regarding money and paying bills: "Is it true that "I" spend too much", and "Who is this "I" that is about to run out of money?"

Step 3. Identify the story you tell yourself that ignites the painful emotion(s).

Stories often are forecasting disaster, perpetuating worry, instilling doubt and obsessing about perfection. These thoughts can cultivate a victim mentality, in which the victim believes that either he or she, or someone else, has been unfairly wronged or injured. An example of a story about the trigger would be, "I don't make enough money to take care of myself and could lose everything if I am not cautious."

Step 4. Feel the emotion of the story you are believing.

Now sincerely ask yourself, "What am I feeling right now?" Since you have identified the causal belief of the stressful thought, take slow deep breaths, placing your attention on any emotions and feelings you are experiencing inside. Place your hand over your heart and tenderly comfort yourself by saying: "Although intense and uncomfortable, this feeling is only temporary. I care very deeply about the vulnerability of my own tender heart."

Step 5. Scan your body.

While still holding your hand over your heart notice the location, intensity and density of the physical feeling in your body, including how sharp or dull the sensation is as you comfort yourself. Continue taking slow deliberate inhales and exhales as you feel the sensations in your body.

Step 6. Acknowledge and accept your feelings.

Accept and know that you are able and willing to handle any arising emotions or sensations, regardless of their intensity. Our minds will interpret intense emotions as wrong and attempt to find distractions to avoid feeling them. The thought "this is too intense" or "I'm overwhelmed" and "I don't want to feel this" is also a story, not the truth of who you are. Reassure yourself of your strength and resilience in surviving any energetic emotional expressions, especially since you are not your emotions, only the observer of them.

Step 7. Connect empathically to understand and validate your experience.

It is essential that we remember that although other people or situations may trigger painful feelings, they can never be the cause of them. The cause of emotional resistance is always the problematic interpretation we make, or the story we are believing about ourselves. But the specific situations or actions that ignited our emotional response can be reinterpreted with awareness. By choosing to think thoughts that calm, empower, and build our confidence, we begin to relax in the peace and wholeness of our true nature. In regard to Step 1, for example, we might think one or all of these thoughts: "I am resourceful and creative; I am open to new opportunities." "I am prosperity itself." "I am the SELF." These sorts of responses allow us to affirm our experience while being compassionate toward our selves.

In summary, thoughts trigger feelings, and feelings communicate critical information on how to successfully navigate our lives in more challenging moments. As we become increasingly aware of the emotions and sensations we are experiencing in response to certain thoughts, we develop greater understanding of the strong connection between our words and self-talk, and our emotions and physical sensations.

With Emotional Self-Awareness we are able to recognize that we are more powerful than we thought we were in overcoming uncomfortable beliefs and 'knee-jerk' responses, by modifying our emotional states. By using ESA and making conscious changes to old patterns of thought, we can shift our awareness to a new way of being or relating. Consciously choosing how we experience life events allows us to stay open to what is happening in the moment and naturally improves the course of our lives, as we become more available to fresh opportunities as they arise.

For a more comprehensive explanation of ESA practice, go to the SoulTranSync Practices Workbook available free for download on the website **www.SoulTranSync.com.**

PART THREE

THE THREE CORE ELEMENTS OF *SOULTRANSYNC™*:

ACCEPTANCE, GRATITUDE AND FORGIVENESS

Introduction to the Three Core Elements

The *SoulTranSync*™ process helps facilitate our awakening journey through embracing the powerful STS Core Elements: Acceptance, Gratitude and Forgiveness. Although these Elements encompass several definitions and beliefs, here each is simply stated as:

Acceptance: When we agree to experience our life as it unfolds (often a negative or uncomfortable situation), without attempting to change it, protest its inevitability, distract ourselves from it, or suppress it.

Gratitude: The quality of being thankful, the readiness to show appreciation for, and the willingness to return to, kindness.

Forgiveness: The deliberate decision to release feelings and stories of resentment or revenge against anyone who has harmed or betrayed us, regardless of whether or not they deserve our forgiveness.

Although spiritual practitioners and theologians have written about and taught the Core Elements used in STS for hundreds of years, the STS practice itself is fresh and innovative. This amalgam of Elements under one umbrella is a radical approach to self-realization that is designed to promote freedom from mental enslavement, to offer sanctuary and clarity from confusion, and to give us peace of mind, whether or not one has a wounded heart. These Elements, when embraced through the STS practice alter us vibrationally, attracting new opportunities, passionate relationships and greater abundance into our lives. The STS Elements cultivate the fertile soil for the heart's awakening and are essential to understanding the power of our Self.

There has never been a better time on Planet Earth, or a greater need for this emancipation of thought, than now. We human beings are uniquely primed to achieve Self-realization at this distinctive moment in history.

Collectively we are rushing through time, absorbing an overabundance of information at the speed of light, which often can leave us feeling isolated and dissatisfied. Our troubled world needs a new paradigm with which to practice, hone, and deepen our resolve to evolve. If we are aware that higher consciousness is a possibility, we can learn to improve our responses to life situations that often feel fragmented and fragile, even threatening, by coming from a clearer place, and seeing through the eyes of conscious awareness.

Even though a single day is still constituted in 24-hour increments, many of us are feeling as if time is speeding up. Since time is an illusion anyway, in truth it can't really be speeding up, but our consciousness perceives that it is. More appears to be happening in less time, in turn producing myriad outcomes for the mind to consider. Having more options to consider can create confusion, doubt and insecurity for the mind, which may alter our human "vibration." Everything in existence revolves around vibration, as molecules and atoms vibrate to create our perception of reality. When these vibrate faster, an illusion of time speeding up is created. Physiologically, our bodies are sensing the speeding up of "something", but our minds are not able to attribute this phenomenon to anything familiar, other than the concept of time.

For example, as a child I had four possible television news options: ABC, CBS, NBC and PBS. Local newspapers generally featured local news, and any information about the world was parceled out to me once daily. But with the introduction of modern media, the breadth of my access to gathering resources and information about the entire world feels as though it has been multiplied by over 1000%! Everyday diverse interpretations of information from multiple media sources are being offered to us, showering our minds with conflicting point of views. We are bombarded constantly with what we are told is vital information from every corner of the world. Our minds are incapable of keeping up with this speed, causing our grasp on our daily lives to feel illusive, *tenuous,* and undependable.

We no longer have the capacity for a clear understanding of our lives, because these lives are always evolving beyond our reason, just out of our grasp. It is for this very reason that what we call "the mind" needs to slow down and pay better attention to the heart. Our hearts don't need news updates and constant access to the lives of our high school friends through social media. Our hearts also don't need the judgments and opinions of so many unqualified commentators and so-called experts, who are always telling us who we are, who we are supposed to be, and what's important to us.

For us to feel courageous, empowered, and free, our hearts require us to stay open to life just as it is. Our hearts want to be unencumbered from fearful interpretations or judgments, especially those of lack and limitation that are intrinsic to how we have been conditioned to think or believe. By living from the intelligence of our hearts instead of our over-stimulated minds, we can inspire more ease in our days, more access to our innate intuition, less stressful living overall, and a more profound sense of our purpose in, and contribution to, the world.

Part One of *Understanding and Embracing Soul Power* provided an extended discussion of Awareness and the Aware Ego Process (AEP). Part Two gives us the Core Practices of STS. Part Three offers the Elements of STS, with practices and examples for living an enlightened existence. The Core Elements are the path to transcending our smaller lives in which there is still suffering, to begin living from the vibration of our hearts, with joy and with gratitude. These Core Elements are infused into the foundation of every STS practice.

Chapter 15

Acceptance Using SoulTranSync

Everything is shown up by being exposed to the light, and whatever is exposed to the light itself becomes ligh

.~ Saint Paul of Taurus Christian

In the classic book *The Power of Now,* Eckhart Tolle states: "*The greatest part of human pain is unnecessary. It is self-created as long as the unobserved mind runs your life*"

The fact is that all suffering is self-created when we don't question the truth of the stories we tell ourselves. The uninquiring, unobservant mind will run your life like an oppressive dictator. The sorrow or upset we create in our lives is always some form of non-acceptance to what is. Our minds are constantly thinking, judging or assessing our lives in some emotionally negative form, and this emotional negativity manifests as *resistance.* Tolle concludes that the amount of suffering in which we languish will depend upon the degree of our resistance to the present moment.[14]

The problem appears to be, that in order to escape painful feelings or strong emotions, our minds continue rejecting, ignoring or denying the circumstances of the present moment. This avoidance leads to some new form of suffering. However, the more we honor and accept the "Now" moment, the more we free ourselves from the torment of the egocentric mind.

Time and Illusion and the Sense of Peace

To avoid the present moment our minds use the illusory state of time—past and future—to feel in control. To the mind, time is ultimately all that exists. It is our infrastructure for organizing and relating to all of life, and consciousness cannot seem to exist without it. Although we need the interaction of time and mind to function in this world, often the two together overtake the spontaneity and creativity of our "one wild and precious life," as poet Mary Oliver has said in her poem, *The Summer Day,*[15] and this can cause us some grief. Our minds continuously seek to maintain control over circumstances, attempting to cover up the present moment with "past" and "future." This illusory relationship with time causes our conscious awareness to be veiled, hiding our infinite imaginations and the source of inspiration that are only present in this Now moment.

By succumbing to the allure of time, and allowing it to be our keeper, we constantly receive misperceptions of reality that can result in suffering. This is the nature of duality, in that our thinking becomes subjective and a "them" and "us" mentality can arise. Along with this aberration of time, our minds may distort or obstruct a clear perception of what our true human nature actually is, one deeply rooted in peaceful co-existence, just like the atomic structure of matter. It is through the cooperation of molecules and cells that our organism exists and is maintained. Once we realize that we have always wanted to live in peace, even while imagining ourselves otherwise at times, our experience can be drawn from the silence, or the emptiness surrounding that peace, and cannot be disturbed by external issues, such as fighting with our minds or with one another.

Peace is already and always Here and Now. Time creates the illusion that Peace is outside of ourselves, or something to "get" or to "win," a product that has a sell-by date and makes us feel separate from each other. This element of time, the need to dominate it, or to eradicate it, or to have it rule right now—is what causes wars. Then when wars end, we call that peace!!

The accumulation of time's effects on our individual and collective mindsets, has resulted in anguish, fear, oppression, poverty, reoccurring wars and more suffering, in our world. Peace itself is causeless, that which engenders lasting happiness in us, and immense freedom in the world. It is the sensation of complete rest. It doesn't happen because we fight for it.

Again, in his classic book, *The Power of Now*, Eckhart Tolle has remarked, *"What could be more insane than to oppose life itself, which is now and always now? Surrender to what is. Say yes to life and see how life suddenly starts working for you rather than against you."*

We are capable of achieving true inner peace when we surrender to what is. Then we see that peace and finding out the truth of who we are, are intrinsic, one to the other. This is how using ESA practice can lead to restoring us to sanity . . . and help us experience that sense of "peace that surpasses all understanding."

Tolle further states that to relieve our suffering and the suffering of others, we should not create any additional time-dependency: *Or at least no more than is necessary to deal with the practical aspects of your life.* In order to stop creating this dependence on time, we must make the present moment the primary focus of our lives, and only pay brief visits to past history or future events, when absolutely required.[16]

Acceptance and Surrender

Our unquestioned egocentric persona has developed protective patterns of thought that allow it to hide from our direct observation. Its resistance to the present moment keeps us distracted and in continual search and rescue of what we need to do, fix or discard. The mind insists on controlling everything, and to maintain its dominance, it relies on obsolete evidence from the past as a reference for what it calls *true,* as well as projected fear thoughts about the future with which to substantiate old patterns of dread and loss.

Acceptance of, and then surrender to, the life of the present moment demands refraining from finding fault, making judgements, or looking for insufficiencies in our current life situation. Egoistic resistance usually creates inner conflict and increases the agony we feel, so our job is to learn to be with what is without these negative energies.

The practice of watching or observing our thoughts without judgment is the beginning of Soul Transcendence. Regular scrutiny of thoughts and the dramas they create, implies accepting them as part of what is occurring at that moment.

We must always come back to this present moment. We focus attention on the feelings within us and our resistance to them, by accepting their existence. If we allow feelings that arise to turn from simple emotions into repetitive thoughts, and over-think the causes of them, we begin judging ourselves, which then shifts the focus away from noticing with awareness what we are feeling. And that is when we lose the present moment. Generating or feeding an identity that is stimulated by mental drama is dangerous and counter-productive to our ultimate freedom. Instead, become aware of what is happening within you, and as difficult as it may be, witness and accept that without a condemning mind.

We learn not to be afraid of feeling anything, no matter how intense or painful. Feeling what is happening right now usually lasts for only a moment, but continuing to identify with it creates ongoing suffering. Most importantly, assume the role of a silent watcher and remain an observer of everything. As we practice discerning who we truly are, apart from our narcissistic mind, we start to experience feelings of empowerment and freedom that are derived from acceptance and surrender.

Sometimes opening up to acceptance of "what is" can carry negative connotations that imply we have given up, or failed to rise to our life's challenges, or that we are weak, or defeated. If this should occur, always remember that true surrender has none of these negative elements.

Acceptance and surrender do not mean we must passively endure, tolerate or withstand whatever the situation in which we find ourselves, is. Rather than viewing these moments as punishment, how can we take positive action and design creative solutions and intentions for ourselves instead?

Surrender is the simple but profound wisdom of yielding to the flow of life instead of opposing its natural path. Remember, surrender does not mean we are giving into the overall situation; rather, we are narrowing our attention to the present moment without mentally labeling it in any way. Non-judgmentalism produces no resistance, and as a result, we don't need to devise yet another negative story to tell our selves.

It's Okay Not to be Okay

Sometimes, acceptance of a challenging situation or emotion feels impossible. When our hearts are closed from hurt and disappointment, or our negative judgment of a situation is unrelenting, "accepting what is" becomes very difficult. But the term "accepting what is" can be misinterpreted. Acceptance doesn't mean that we agree with the person who wronged us, or the circumstances that did not go in our favor. Nor is acceptance an endorsement of distasteful actions or behaviors. Accepting does not dismiss or dishonor our feelings of loss or grief; nor does it mean that we just give up what we desire or see.

Acceptance of reality is acknowledgment, without judgment, of *how you feel* about a person or situation that occurs. A better phrase than "I accept" may be, "It's OK.'" Being okay with ourselves, even our resistance, is the meaning of true Self-acceptance. It's okay not to be okay. For example, "It's OK that I feel angry because my boss takes credit for my work." Or "It's OK that I feel jealous because my friend is more popular than I am." Or "It's OK that I resent my sister because she takes advantage of me."

The conscious resignation that our perceptions are real to us, and that our feelings about them are also not wrong, supports *peaceful awareness*. What we feel can never be wrong, and by realizing our feelings without judgment we allow ourselves to express our emotions, feel them deeply, and then, with practice, release them. This helps us to move beyond the person or circumstance that has contributed to the felt sense that we are locked in an emotional trap. Because we have not made ourselves wrong for our feelings, we are poised to avoid unnecessary guilt and shame. In addition, because we have not made another person or situation wrong, we can lovingly interrupt a story or pattern of ours that has had a negative energy of its own and has played over and over within us, without our awareness.

Being Lovingly Present with Our Selves

As a generalization, we are all more comfortable with perpetual optimism, or responding affirmatively by showing up and smiling no matter what. We also get uncomfortable seeing others in pain, so in order to maintain good will, we often hide our own distress. The schools of the "Law of Attraction" and positive thinking endorse overcoming fear, remaining strong enough to push past our discomfort, and replace our thinking with positive thoughts. Hypothetically, this good advice seems like the appropriate way to handle resistance, pain and disappointment, but sometimes this forced optimism can trap us in a cycle of shame and guilt.

The decision to choose positivity as our general attitude and posture can be incredibly empowering, especially when our hearts and minds are open to it. But when we are not feeling strong and confident, what do we do with those feelings? While stuck in a funky emotion, afraid of an outcome, or saddened by an experience, where do we go to lick our wounds until we get to a better, easier place?

Although optimism has its place, there is no substitute for accepting and staying lovingly present with our stressful feelings. Emotional Self Awareness is a response that supports the practice of self-compassion. It also nurtures genuine inner exploration and encourages authentic self-expression. How able we are to relate kindly toward ourselves, especially when our innocence feels threatened or we are wounded, is the foundation of Soul Transcendence; nurturing self-compassion and self-forgiveness are its ideals.

Chapter 16

Acceptance as Flow

Every moment of every day, this life can feel like one miracle after another is revealing itself to us. This is living in a synchronistic Flow, when each day is met with less stress and resistance, and more passion and success. Best of all, this Flow requires no struggle or strain to accomplish.

There is already a harmonizing Flow to life that guides us toward the effortless fulfillment of our heart's desires. Whether we are conscious of it or not, this flow occurs continuously. Our great challenge is learning how to recognize and cooperate with Flow, instead of blocking or restricting our experience of it.

There are three fundamental decisions that we can make right out of the gait to start living life in that synchronistic Flow. All of these decisions are rudimentary, but require committed awareness.

1. Flowing with the Unknown

The first decision to make is to be willing to let go of what we "think" we know. Most perceptions we have about everything are bogus or inaccurate. In other words, we must stop forcing things to go the way we think they should be. Once we allow ourselves to be completely honest about what we "think we know", we discover that most of our facts are half-truths, false rumors, assumptions, or fantasies. Or, we find that we have used incomplete data to make inaccurate conclusions. And sometimes, we even believe outright lies.

> *In other words, we need to stop trying to force things to go the way we think they should, because of what we think we know.*

Our egocentric mind is always looking for validation, a way to proclaim our self-righteousness. We may feel threatened by someone or something that does not align with the positions we've adopted. We can observe this most profoundly when considering how ethnicity, family, religion and politics are viewed on an individual or collective basis. Each of these viewpoints boxes us into a system of beliefs and behaviors that may often obscure the blessings inherent in our life's flow.

This is not to suggest that we completely ignore what we consider factual, but rather, that we consider the possibility that what our conditioning tells us is a fact may actually be a limited or incorrect point of view. These perceived "facts" may be fallacious and better taken with a giant grain of salt. What we understand to be truthful or adequate information may be nothing more than cleverly disguised misinformation.

Detachment from clinging to our conditioned opinions is vital in suspending judgments and becoming more open-minded. Open-mindedness is a preferred state of consciousness that allows for new and sometimes inspired perceptions to occur. By its nature, we are able to move from a defiant or unwilling space to a more harmonious state, congruent with the way we wish to live our lives.

The opportunity to stimulate Flow often helps fulfill our heart's desires in a way far different, and infinitely better, than anything we could ever imagine. And to be in a natural flow with life, we don't need to understand or control the mystery of the Unknown, because our true SELF is unknown. Our direct and immediate experiences naturally unfold in boundless Conscious Awareness, and are merely momentary, short-lived phenomena, arising and passing away, in and as, the enigmatic aliveness of the Unknown.

Nisargadatta Maharaj, an Indian spiritual teacher and philosopher of Advaita Vedanta, is still considered one of the most insightful of teachers of Non-duality. In the 1973 publication of his most famous book, "I AM THAT", he expresses the core of all his communication in a few brilliant sentences:

I do not negate the world.
I see it as appearing in consciousness,
which is the totality of the known
in the immensity of the Unknown.[17]

2. Flowing with Intuition

The second decision for living life in a harmonious Flow requires paying attention!

Flow constantly guides us toward effortless fulfillment of our desires, but to reap these rewards, we want to remain open and receptive to the subtle ways Flow may attempt to lead us.

By paying close attention to what's going on in our lives, we can continuously receive direction from our own intuition. Intuition is our most valuable and reliable source of guidance, an inner and instinctive mechanism, a "knowing," without a logical thought process. Intuition can be experienced as an "inner voice," but the degree of its strength may vary depending upon one's level of consciousness. Our inner voices share loving, nurturing, and courageous insights and cellular information with us, and can guide us away from circumstances or people that are not in our best interests. Sometimes intuition will arouse new and empowered approaches to meeting our lives and the choices that are presented to us. But if our consciousness is buried under guilt and shame, our intuition will also be affected. The gift of guidance can sometimes be corrupted by fear, and the inner voice may be stifled by imagined terrors, projections, or impending calamities, which then may be expressed as desperate cries for protection or help.

True intuition is usually aware of the next right step to take, and it seeks to tell us what that step might be. To hear what our intuition wants to tell us, it is important that we take the time to slow down, get quiet, and listen to that still, small voice. By intentionally honoring and respecting the guidance we receive when we hear it, we build our spiritual muscles and remain faithful to the concept of the perfection of Flow, as it manifests in our lives, in alliance with our true nature, which always seeks peace.

3._Flowing with Resilience

When we are knocked down, slowed down, or Flow is obstructed, we can see how easily that can affect our level of resilience. This is the third decision we must make.

There is a perfect television commercial called "Taylor vs. Treadmill" that demonstrates the beauty of flowing with resilience. This commercial is selling Apple Music and stars young pop star Taylor Swift. In this scene Taylor is choosing music from her cell phone to accompany her workout on the treadmill. She chooses a hip hop song by the rapper Drake, a hard beat that does not appear to be the sound this Country Music Princess would listen to. She stretches her body, jumps on the treadmill and begins her workout. Taylor immediately finds her groove in the music, lip-syncing the lyrics and imitating the rapper's performance. We can feel her getting caught up, even inspired, by the rhythmic beat and rawness of the music. She assumes the attitude and expression of the music and gets lost in the flow of her work out.

All of a sudden she misses a step in her run on the moving treadmill, slides off the belt, and falls flat on her face, hard. For a brief moment she lies face down on the floor. Most of us would have been physically and emotionally devastated by this sudden trauma, but Taylor doesn't miss a beat! Demonstrating "resilient Flow" Taylor immediately regains her musical groove, pulls herself off the floor and returns back to her workout.

Although this is an extreme example of resilience, I love seeing this pop star take a hard blow, then quickly recover, returning back to her bliss. Highly successful people are generally known for their resilience. Most of them believe that life will have hard, painful moments; but how quickly they recover determines how available or open they can be to more opportunities, success and happiness.

Resilience is the process of adapting and bending in the face of adversity, trauma, tragedy, threats, or any significant sources of stress. Strong resilience is essential when facing challenges in our family and intimate relationships, serious health problems, or workplace and financial stressors. Our elasticity and ability to bounce back from difficult experiences is demonstrated in how open and flexible we are to accepting life as it is.

Resilience does not mean that a person doesn't experience difficulties or distress. The pathway to resilience may involve considerable emotional anguish. Even Taylor took a moment to acknowledge the fall, and the blow she took to her groove. But she also maintained flexibility and balance in the face of stressful circumstances and traumatic events.

Everyone has the capacity to develop this kind of Flow. To build personal resilience we allow ourselves to experience and acknowledge our strong emotions, move forward to undertake the wise actions to deal with our problems, and step back when necessary to rest and to re-energize our vision of who we wish to be. After stressful moments, we regain support and encouragement by taking care of ourselves, with compassionate nurturing, self-love and appreciation.

In summary, please remember, it is instrumental to let go of what we "think" we know if we are searching for our own Flow. Also, we Flow by trusting our intuition and paying closer attention to what is here and now, which often will call a halt to the idea of trying to force things to go the way we think they should. By our willingness to develop resilience in case of a set-back, we can be better equipped for a quick recovery. As we attune to these suggestions, we will begin to live a life that is dramatically more fulfilling, immensely more joyful, and, remarkably effortless.

This new approach to acceptance may require some practice, and I encourage you to do some of the Acceptance Exercises in the *SoulTranSync*™ Workbook.

We may try accepting small things first and then move on to those difficult or annoying challenges. But once we master acceptance, we quickly return to our natural state of peace and general well-being.

CHAPTER 17

GRATITUDE USING SOULTRANSYNC™

Let us rise up and be thankful, for if we didn't learn a lot today, at least we learned a little, and if we didn't learn a little, at least we didn't get sick, and if we got sick, at least we didn't die; so, let us all be thankful.

~ Anonymous.

The simple phrase "Thank you" is an extraordinary statement. No other phrase has the transformative power that this simple declaration of gratitude has. To thank is to express appreciation. When people feel appreciation, which feels like an actual force field, their minds, heart, and bodies are positively charged with an energy that can be used to transform daily lives.

If the only prayer you ever say in your entire life is 'thank you', it will be enough.[18]

~ Meister Eckhart

The energy of appreciation can invigorate relationships, enhance productivity at work, revitalize health and aging, ignite prosperity, and even ward off crises.

The soul-nurturing practice of gratitude is the key to unlocking our grace and cultivating a more rewarding perspective on life. When we allow ourselves to feel the warmth and kindness of such appreciation, it is naturally complemented by an elevation in heart-awareness, and the broadening of one's perspective. The more our life expands, the more our sense of gratitude develops, so a reinforcing cycle is created. When heart-centered gratitude is cultivated, we learn to feel appreciation even for the problems we face in life. To be able to reflect back on our struggles with appreciation is proof of expanding awareness. Accepting severe hardships or disappointments with a sense of gratitude that is embedded in faith of a lasting triumph (even if this moment does not feel that way), is an expression of enlightened awareness.

Gratitude is also the joyful recognition that our lives are blessed with countless resources that support and maintain our existence.

The old maxim to "count one's blessings" may seem trite, but in times of distress a sense of gratitude for what is good in our lives can ground us and give us the backbone we need for enduring or overcoming difficulties. Gratitude can be the key to unlocking a more open and rewarding perspective, as feelings of appreciation are often accompanied by an elevation in the state of our lives. In other words, there is no room for an ego when we feel appreciation. In that place, we are, each of us, all Heart.

In turn, the consequence of ingratitude is the arrogant delusion that we are detached and separate from each other and our world. Not being aware of the reality of our mutual interdependence makes us victim to destructive impulses. Greed and envy are what we humans often experience when we are not recognizing our Oneness and owning our gratitude for it.

We all have met or know people who act ungratefully. They frequently believe that their needs and desires are all that matters in the world. These people carry a heaviness in their energetic essence, and can sometimes trigger feelings of exhaustion, boredom, irritation, stress, anxiety, threat, overwhelm or depression just after a few moments in their company.

We sometimes call them "energy vampires" because they make us feel tired or emotionally drained when we're around them. Their stories usually are about lack or limitation and can appeal to our need to help others. Relationships with ungrateful people can trigger our own vulnerability. Therefore, it is important that we make an effort to discern the underpinnings of those relationships that appear as unloving to us and take note of their energetic expressions.

Noticing this in someone else may be a message to us. When we recognize what the message is, we can be grateful that this behavior of theirs triggered us and made us more aware.

When we honor life and act with a sense of appreciation, we are aligning ourselves energetically and vibrationally with the core direction of the cosmos. The concept of "vibrational match" is an important theme expressed in most Law of Attraction teachings. Vibrational match can be understood as "like attracts like."

Whether we want to realize it or not, we are responsible for bringing both positive and negative effects into our lives. Where we place our focus and our emotional energies has an intense and direct impact on what happens to us. More simply said, "What we think about is what we are creating." The practice of gratitude helps us to consciously be aware of our good fortune, placing our focus more on what we do want to see in our lives, instead of what we want to avoid. True gratitude supports that which enhances, and opposes that which diminishes, giving us a genuine tool for reflection on life in all its fullness.

In Search of Continual Gratitude

To be consciously grateful means to be in continual search and assessment of opportunities in our lives to express our appreciation. The following is a list of questions that are often overlooked when counting our blessings. Take a moment and answer these questions for yourself. My responses to these questions have brought about genuine and more enlightened perspectives on the blessed nature of my life. I hope they open your heart in the same way.

- **What are the friendships and relationships I am most thankful for?**

  Include here especially the people you might generally overlook, e.g., relatives, co-workers.

  Example: Once both my parents had died, I found myself neglecting my father's sister, my Aunt Vivian. She played an important role in my youth by tutoring me every weekend in math, the subject area I was challenged by most. My aunt was a busy teacher with five children of her own, but she regularly made special time for me.

Thank you, Aunt Vivian, for your patience and care for me. I will always appreciate your love for me.

- **In retrospect, what have I overlooked in the past year that I am most grateful for?**

Was there an accomplishment, or even a failure, that you may have forgotten to appreciate?

We all can, in retrospective moments, recall when we have overlooked expressing our gratitude. For example: I injured myself recently at the gym and experienced some real discomfort. I am now aware that although the pain I experienced slowed me down, it also allowed me to be more present and available for the love, tenderness, and compassion I received from my wife in my vulnerability.

Thank you to my wife for loving and caring for me when I am in pain and feel hurt.

- **What activities in my life do I feel grateful for?**

Have you sometimes overlooked little things, taking them for granted?

Example: I spent my adult life jogging, swimming, eating well and supplementing my diet with many health products to ward off illness. People often complimented me on my healthy, youthful appearance. In my early 50s I began experiencing progressive pain in my legs and back. This unrelenting pain went on for years and affected my self-esteem. I was no longer a strong, vital and healthy man. I felt angry and ashamed of the state of my physical existence. I went from running 10k races to, within a few years, needing my wife to push me around in a wheel chair. Because of my disability, my once active world became smaller and more difficult to manage. It got so bad that I believed I needed major back surgery to walk again.

The surgery turned out badly, and afterwards I was in even more pain. I began losing hope of ever returning back to the strong, capable and adventurous man I had always been. One day I decided to end all of the pain therapy and pills and return to the pool. Being in the water I was able to begin my rehabilitation. Walking the pool was a powerful therapeutic process that inspired solitude and introspection. It allowed me to be present with myself and focus on all the things I was grateful for.

As I began to see how blessed I was to enjoy the simple movements I was capable of in the pool, my body began to respond to this appreciation. I soon became grateful for my entire body from head to toe, identifying each and every part inside and outside for which I could give love and appreciation. I am now able to walk for long periods, my stride is stronger, and I am no longer in pain.

Thank you for the magnificent durability and agility of my physical body; even in pain it services me well.

- **What insights have I gained that allow me to feel more grateful in my life?**

  Our personal insights are the by-product of greater awareness. Awareness expands as our judgments are cleared from consciousness.

Like many, I believed that I had strengths and weaknesses, or in other words, abilities and lack of abilities. I felt that I should be valued and appreciated for my more robust abilities and forgiven for those in which I was frail. I spent most of life avoiding situations that made me feel vulnerable or exposed as "not good enough." Public speaking was my kryptonite. It made me feel clumsy, inarticulate and awkward. Once I stopped believing that the uncomfortable and embarrassing feeling that public speaking evoked in me was wrong, I began enjoying the thrill of being openly vulnerable to it.

Thank you for the awareness that I cannot be wrong, or "not enough" when I am able to be vulnerable.

Every day we meet someone who brings support, awareness or empathy to our day at just the perfect moment. My elderly mother had been very sick with heart disease for a long time, but she wanted to come and visit me in Florida during the holidays. I was thrilled to have my mother with me, but I was reluctant to take her away from the reliable medical care and support she had in Chicago. The plane ride to Florida was very hard on her heart.

As soon as she arrived, she began having severe heart failure and was hospitalized. This was the most frightening moment of my life. Seeing my mother so sick and helpless made me feel desperate and vulnerable. The day before she was to be released from the hospital and back into my care, I felt complete panic. I was sitting in my car in a mini-mall parking lot and worrying about how I was going to care for my sick mother. I had no experience in caring for my mother in this state, but knew I had to figure it out. All I could do was pray for guidance.

For some reason, at that moment, I looked across the parking lot and saw a furniture store and was "called" to visit it. As soon as I walked in the store I began sharing my situation with the saleswoman. I told her that my mother would be out of the hospital the next day, and I didn't know what to do.

This woman was my angel. She started out by selling me a recliner chair for my mother to sit in so that her feet could be elevated, and then made wonderful recommendations of agencies and other resources that would assist me with her care. I left the store that morning feeling more prepared and hopeful. Now I had a plan for my mother's arrival from the hospital the next day. What grace!

> *Thank you, store clerk, for being my angel, and blessing me with the miracle of perfect timing.*

Gratitude as Awareness: A Song

In the 90's there was a popular song that I loved, written and performed by musical artist Alanis Morissette. The name of the song was simply called "Thank U." This song was Morissette's reaction to the conflicted feelings she had experienced after achieving enormous and rapid success. In her VH1 *Storytellers* appearance, she explained:

> *I felt that I lived in a culture that told me that I had to consistently and constantly look outside myself to feel this elusive bliss. And I achieved a lot of what society had told me to achieve and I still didn't feel peaceful. I started questioning everything, and I realized that actually everything was an illusion and it was scary for me because everything I had believed*

> *in was dissolving in front of me and there was a death of sorts, a really beautiful one ultimately, but at first a very scary one, and so I stopped. I stopped for the first time and I was overcome with a huge sense of compassion for myself first, and then naturally that translated into my feeling and compassion for everyone around me and a huge amount of gratitude that I had never felt before to this extent.*

What makes this song so special is how Morisette expresses gratitude and awareness through sharing her challenges and vulnerability. I found I could immediately relate on a personal level to her song, and at the same time, the message was fully universal, for everyone. I suggest you check out this inspiring music video on YouTube:
https://www.youtube.com/watch?v=OOgpT5rEKIU. Here is how this powerful song of gratitude has inspired my own introspection and awareness.

The first line of the song is "**How 'bout getting off all these antibiotics?"**

My life has shown me that my physical and emotional wellness are interrelated, and that my dependency on cures and healings outside of myself are just illusionary remedies. Once I stopped searching the world for antidotes I became grateful in the awareness that only I am the cure.

"How 'bout stopping eating when I'm full up?"

As I seek objects for comfort in my belief of insufficiency and unworthiness, there is never enough. Overindulgence in life's pleasures was once my way of numbing the feeling of emptiness. When I became fully aware of SELF, I was no longer lost in the desires of the mind.

"How 'bout them transparent dangling carrots?"

This can refer to anything that motivates you, even though you can't see it as motivation, and leads you to a path of Self-Awareness. In the song, she gives thanks to things like terror, disillusionment, frailty, consequence (karma), and silence. Each of these were motivational "carrots" that have inspired my own emotional awareness and spiritual growth.

"How 'bout that ever elusive kudo?"

A kudo is praise or acknowledgement of a job well done. My mind sometimes craves hearing compliments about what I've done or how much I have accomplished, but lately I have also become grateful for an intangible and indefinable love of Self, that does not need outside praise.

"How 'bout me not blaming you for everything?"

This line is a kind of 'self-talk', that awakens awareness in me of the responsibility I have for my own perceptions. I have learned to let myself off the hook and not be victimized by my own misperceptions. When I mislead myself with blame and judgment, it only supports me in ignoring the awareness of SELF/Self. I am grateful for the awareness that "you" only exist as a reflection back to Self, and that not blaming or judging "you" for anything is a demonstration of Self-love.

"How 'bout me enjoying the moment for once?"

By appreciating the present moment completely and thoroughly, I can no longer regret what I thought I did, or didn't do, in the past. I feel grateful for the present moment deterring me from planning or fearing what's going to happen in the future.

"How 'bout how good it feels to finally forgive you?"

Non-duality teaches that there is no other, and that the "you" that is mentioned is only an illusion of separation. I forgive myself for forgetting the peace and bliss of my true nature. I now remember with gratitude the wholeness of Self.

"How 'bout grieving it all one at a time?"

Grieving, in this sense, is the very human expression of moving through resistance to loss or change, which may result in unresolved sadness, or the feelings of lack, as if something were missing. As my resistance eventually bubbled up to the surface, it caused me to face each story of loss or separation, one story at a time, through my heart. By allowing myself to feel emotions as they arose, I was free to un-tether my soul, respond directly, and could then choose love in that moment, however that then looked to me. My life is a continual evolutionary cycle of resistance, then awareness, one story at a time. Because I am grateful for the deep emotions and memories that return back to me, instead of loss, I can experience gratitude and remember Morisette's words . . .

> ***The moment I let go of it was the moment . . . I got more than I could handle. The moment I jumped off of it . . . was the moment I touched down.***

Once we really let go of our ego's belief in separation and duality, we are incredibly liberated, free. We experience a wellspring of happiness and energy, even more than we can handle. Generally speaking, we cling to our stories, even when the stories keep us small and afraid. By letting go and surrendering to life as it is, we awaken to the perfection of the Self. I have cried long and hard; not from sadness, but from gratitude for the incredible joy I received from letting it all go, whatever it was, and being alive to the NOW moment.

"How 'bout no longer being masochistic? How 'bout remembering your divinity?"

We are all masochistic when we suffer pain and degradation that is self-imposed or appears to be imposed by others. I am grateful that I am a living, breathing divine being, a soul with a body here on Earth. I don't need or deserve anyone's abuse, especially my own self-abuse.

"How 'bout unabashedly bawling your eyes out?"

When your mind is ripe and your heart is open, tears will come naturally, freely and in abundance. Whenever I have allowed myself an unapologetic expression of sincerity, tears arise, in gratitude. This always inspires an outpouring of "love awareness" in my field of consciousness. I am thankful for this beautiful and powerful response to my vulnerability.

"How 'bout not equating death with stopping?"

Simply put, the physical death of this current body is not absolute death. The body is the vehicle we incarnate into but our real selves are spirit. A quote from Zen Master Seung Sahn states, "If you can break the wall of yourself, you will become infinite in time and space."[19] I am grateful and comforted to know that with the confrontation of the smaller egoic self, a kind of death occurs, and the Love that I am can be felt as eternal and everlasting. This experience is like "dying before we die" so that when we leave this body, we know that Love remains.

Cultivate the habit of being grateful for every good thing that comes to you, and to give thanks continuously.
And because all things have contributed to your advancement, you should include all things in your gratitude.[20]

~ Ralph Waldo Emerson

Chapter 18

Forgiveness Using SoulTranSync

Spiritual Forgiveness

If in truth we are all One, then the foundation of all forgiveness comes down to Self-forgiveness. When we have hurt or damaged someone, we are inevitably only hurting our self. But it must also be true that when we forgive another, we simultaneously forgive ourselves. When forgiveness comes from our spiritual capacity to love and understand human nature, it doesn't require human judgment and "victim consciousness," only our emotional intelligence. This is because our evolving souls continually attract people and circumstances into our field of consciousness that push our buttons and trigger the parts of ourselves that we dislike, hide, or disown. These parts of us are repressed, denied and often projected onto others, and mirror our own internal emotional resistance. It certainly can be difficult to understand why we would invite all of the problematic relationships into our lives specifically for the purpose of forgiving ourselves!

Forgiveness is made a whole lot easier once we realize that forgiving others is a way of releasing the unconscious judgment we hold against ourselves. Thus, we give ourselves a pseudo-replacement to forgive, as a representative of our own self.

"Spiritual" forgiveness teaches us that there are no accidents, and no one is doing anything wrong, or making any mistake. Life is always presenting us with what we need for our soul's evolution, so in truth, there are no victims and no perpetrators to blame.

We see the present moment only as the perfect expression of life as it is. At the core of spiritual forgiveness is simply forgiving ourselves. Spiritual forgiveness is an introspective approach to forgiveness.

Introspection (from the Inside, Out) vs. Extrospection (from the Outside, In)

Your visions will become clear
only when you can look into your own heart.
Who looks outside, dreams; who looks inside, awakens.

~C.G Jung

Introspection and extrospection relate to different levels of our attention's focus. The word introspection is defined as the observation or examination of our own mental and emotional state, mental processes, and so on. It is the act of looking within oneself, as opposed to extrospection, which is observation, consideration and understanding of things outside of our self, or the examination and study of the world's effect on us.

Introspection (Inside out) is exploring one's beliefs, conscious thoughts, and feelings. In psychology the process of introspection relies exclusively on our own observation of our mental, emotional and spiritual states. With Introspection we are able to become aware of our triggers, our underlying beliefs, the fears, the perspectives and the values that drive our behaviors.

> ***Being able to introspect is empowering.***

Extrospection (Outside in) is the observation of things external to, or outside of, one's own mind, as distinct from introspection, which is the direct observation of the mind's internal processes. Extrospection uses the ordinary five-senses for perception, and uses reasoning concerning the things perceived.

> ***Awareness of our external environment helps make informed decisions, but also may demonstrate our inability to see the forest for the trees.***

Conventional Forgiveness

While conventional forgiveness calls upon the finest of human qualities and characteristics, such as mercy, tolerance, humility, kindness and most of all, the exercise of compassion, it has no "spiritual" context. Although these inspiring qualities are recognized and honored in the world of humanity, the nature of our human mind suggests judgment and condemnation first before forgiveness.

Conventional forgiveness is based in duality, first polarizing everything as right or wrong, good or bad, enough or not enough. For example, if I am going on an important business trip, and on the way to the airport the traffic is not moving fast enough to get me to my flight on time, my first thought is "I should have left for the airport earlier." I'm immediately assuming I've made the wrong choice to leave when I did. Another example would be that I got busy at work and forgot to pick up my mother from the doctor. By my forgetting this, she ended up having to take a cab home. I can feel that I am a neglectful son, as a result. This attitude assumes that I have done the wrong thing, that I should have paid better attention to time.

In this same scenario, my mother also believes that forgetting to pick her up is proof that I don't care for her. She not only feels I'm wrong for forgetting to retrieve her from the doctor, but that this neglect supports her belief of my general disregard of her. These examples demonstrate that when we experience unwanted or unexpected situations, our general tendency is to harshly judge ourselves and others for our feelings, loss, or pain. This judgment often turns into relentless assessments of imperfection and unworthiness, fostering victim consciousness within us.

Victim consciousness is an unhappy story that we believe about ourselves. It prompts us to see the world as the cause of our misery and leaves us feeling at the mercy of those who "make us feel bad," "hold us back," or hurt, abuse, or control us. When we are experiencing victim consciousness, we are emphasizing that we have been wronged and that something *bad* has to be endured. Therefore, the perpetrator of the wrong act is deemed responsible for the pain or loss we are feeling.

The following is a short list of common beliefs that hold us in victim consciousness and hinder our ability to forgive ourselves:

- **"Things are just not the way they should be."**

This limiting belief is common to us, and most often the source of human suffering. It causes us to become preoccupied with problems, instead of seeing the potential opportunities we have in front of us. Without awareness, this thought compels us to renounce or attack the things (or persons) we believe should be different from the way in which we perceive them.

- **"They shouldn't be allowed to get away with the awful things they do."**

This self-righteous belief gives our minds reasons or causes to act with justified vengeance. Thoughts of punishment or retribution follow. Then when we believe someone has unjustifiably subjected us to their will, or unabashedly attempted to manipulate us or things, exclusively in their favor. But in reality, injustices are performed by people, just like you and me, who believe their own thinking is the standard for the way life should be.

- **"These things shouldn't have happened to me."**

Believing this is true hinders our awareness of the perfection of our lives, just as it is. Even in moments of great pain and resistance there is not a single thing that has happened to you that has not been vital for your life purpose and growth.

The word "should" is always in resistance to reality. Peace of mind and freedom never come from the demand that things be different than the way they are. Spiritual forgiveness leads us to a renewed perspective of our resistance, by opening us up to a fresh interpretation of life, based on the spiritual reality that everything happens for a reason.

Self-Forgiveness Instead of Conventional Forgiveness

Self-forgiveness, combined with introspection, can become our most valuable practice for healing emotional trauma, by just redirecting our attention back to the Self. Self-acceptance, self-compassion and especially self-love are all by-products of self-forgiveness. Until we are willing to introspect, and bring genuine forgiveness to ourselves, we are severed from the truth of our original nature and subject to the false belief that we are a separate self. This belief is at the core of all our suffering. To transcend this erroneous belief, we want to generate enough love and forgiveness toward ourselves, and at the same time, open our hearts to a more sacred, or mystical, alignment with Self.

It is difficult to understand that sometimes withholding forgiveness from one's self is actually motivated by love. Many of us feel we've done things that make us unforgivable, and in the hope that we will never do those things again, we hold ourselves hostage. We make ourselves responsible, so as to not hurt anyone else or even ourselves, again. This lack of self-forgiveness is usually unconscious.

For many years my Shadow identity of unworthiness protected me from disappointment and rejection by lowering my expectations of myself. But at the same time that shadow self sold me short by guarding my unconscious shame and guilt. Withholding self-forgiveness caused me to feel separate and cut me off from loving my larger or higher Self, and as a result I often acted in the same ways that I had held myself unforgivable for, in the first place! This is because I carried the energy of "I BELIEVE I am unworthy" in my energy field, thereby attracting life circumstances that reflected what I thought were TRUE about myself.

There Are No Regrets, Because I've Done Nothing Wrong

To practice self-forgiveness, first, let's take a look at past experiences where the result was reinforced guilt or shame. When we get in touch with those moments again, we realize that our truest intention was to take care of ourselves in the best way we knew at that time. By seeing the experience through such limited points of view, we made choices that brought us undesirable results, but we were always doing the best we could.

Through self-forgiveness we are able to accept the truth that at each challenging moment of our lives we can only be aware of what we are aware of at that given moment. To be punished or kept "on the hook" for not having conscious awareness is self-abuse. Our reactions and behaviors during vulnerable moments, when we judge harshly, are only because they come from a basic human instinct to survive. The nature of this survival instinct is based on self-love, even though we may be feeling its "flight or fight" aspect.

Every human heart deserves redemption, freedom from the bondage of a tormented mind. But this requires paying a ransom, a price that makes redemption possible. The price or sacrifice is the willingness to Self-forgive our alleged trespasses.

In Truth, we are not flawed humans unable to overcome our basic animal nature; instead we are the heartfelt manifestation of Love. If we have done something that could be perceived as cruel or evil to another, or committed acts of violence toward someone else, it is even possible to forgive ourselves for those "unforgivable" actions.

Self-forgiveness is also appropriate even when someone has undertaken such terrible actions against others, such as murder, or killing someone in a war, if the person is willing to look inside and see into their motives at the time. They may realize that they believed that their actions would make their situation or someone else's better at the time, or that they were doing the best they could under the circumstances, like following orders. This can be seen as an attempt to take care of (or love) themselves the only way they knew how, in that moment. This is true for all of us, for all of our actions.

Although I'm not condoning any act that causes suffering, I am bringing awareness to the truth that anything that we've done is forgivable when we look deeply and honestly into our hearts. In our essential natures, our actions are inherently driven by the desire to love ourselves as best we can.

How I Learned to Forgive Myself

I once was persuaded by a very close friend of mine to invest in a small printer ink refill business. He convinced me that the investment was solid and that he and I would work the business together as partners. I would oversee operations and he would create the sales leads. This idea of refilling and selling used ink cartridges sounded profitable and even fun. In the past, for every business I had ever started, I was the sole investor and carried the all the responsibility on my shoulders. I saw this venture as an opportunity to make some extra money in a business that was light and easy, and because I had a partner who knew how to produce sales I felt that it would be a lucrative collaboration.

At that time, I was already overwhelmed by running four non-profit businesses, three charter schools and a community after-school golf program, and my for-profit management company that oversaw everything. All of these businesses had many moving parts and carried tremendous responsibilities. I wanted something simple, straightforward and effortless in my life to help make up for the heaviness I felt inside.

This particular franchise business would cost me seventy-five thousand dollars to purchase. The expense was to be split between the two of us. We would also need to lease space for both retail and manufacturing. Since I had experience running many types of small enterprises, my partner let me take the lead in making all of the operational decisions. I accepted that would be a fair exchange, since I was also busy running my other businesses. I was looking forward to him taking the lead in generating sales, which I believed to be my weakness. Although my friend had never run a business of his own, I knew him to be a strong salesman in his other occupations.

Soon after building the facility and adding the machinery, hiring staff and launching the business, my partner simply disappeared. I mean he fell off the face of the earth! I called him many times with no response, not even a text message. I soon realized that he was MIA (missing in action). I was greatly hurt and disappointed that my friend had abandoned our dream of working together toward a common intent, but most of all I was just ashamed of how stupid I had been to take on the responsibility of this new business. I had only agreed to invest in this venture in the first place because I thought he would be sharing the adventure with me. And now I was forced to take on this burden all alone. I started seeing myself as a victim again, like in my Christmas story, and that my needs and desires were not important to someone else. I was angry and hurt, believing that I had been disregarded, and was now forced to assume the role of salesman too.

Since I had developed such good will in the community, I thought this was a good place to start in order to develop my client base and remedy the situation I found myself in. Truthfully, I hated it. Promising people that they would save money by buying their ink and toner from me was embarrassing and humiliating, but I did it anyway.

I was in such resistance to this business, but I tried to keep up a good face. The two young employees I hired to manufacture the refills and run the retail were enthusiastic about the opportunity. I hoped their outlook would inspire me and soothe my secret feelings of contempt and disappointment that I held for the business.

After a year of performing at minimal effort and barely breaking even from my sales efforts, I had to call it quits and shut down the business. I felt deep shame and guilt for what I believed was failure. I had invested a substantial amount of money, manpower and time in a venture that I never wanted to be in, and I was embarrassed at how quickly I wanted to give up and shut down everything. But the business was just making me sick.

Looking back on this moment I am now able to see that this business was a perfect opportunity for me to gain awareness of myself through self-forgiveness. Even though this small failure was just a blip on the scale of the success of my other enterprises, I allowed it to color my whole life, and suffered the feelings of being unsuccessful about everything I was doing. I felt out of control. I now am able to see that even my motivation for this business collaboration was a call to self-love: I believed that investing in our friendship through this business would bring great healing to both of us and enhance our connection.

I have since forgiven myself for my anger and disappointment in the way he abandoned our partnership. Just like that Christmas morning when I allowed myself to be taken advantage of by my parents without receiving recognition from them. In return, the pain I felt then poisoned any positive feelings I had for all my businesses.

In time, I began to forgive myself by accepting that my truest purpose for pursuing this business investment was not money but love, the love of friendship, the love of creating an opportunity with someone, and the love of Self.

As it turned out, I eventually discovered that my so-called business partner had experienced an emotional breakdown over the loss of his mother and was unable to reveal to me the pain he suffered because of her death. After reconnecting years later, he shared that he had wanted to believe that our partnership would help him through his depression, but then he realized he wasn't feeling strong enough to face a new venture, and he didn't want to let me down. He had his wounds too.

I have forgiven myself for believing that what happened was proof of personal failure. I was stuck in a limiting belief about myself, that I was no salesman, and I let the team down by not producing enough sales to sustain the business. In addition, I had wasted money on a business that I had absolutely no interest in, or vision for, in the first place.

I am able to see now that I was going through a vulnerable time in my life, searching for a nurturing space in which to feel enthusiasm and success. My Charter School management company had become difficult and problematic, and I felt I needed something that was light and fun to take my attention off the weight on my shoulders. That's why I entered into that ink replacement business to begin with. Even though the experience increased stress and challenged my self-esteem, I was only doing the best I knew how to care for myself in that moment.

Self-forgiveness has helped me see into the purity of my own heart and become aware of the reasons why I had sabotaged myself. In my healing of this incident I was able to look back and see how—given what I know now—I would have done things differently. However, as I see why I suffered for my mistakes, I can apply self-forgiveness, and by letting go of the burdens of the past, I can stop beating myself up for my perceived failings.

Greater self-awareness is the gift and by-product of self-forgiveness. Once I saw my habitual patterns, how I stacked up condemnations and judgments upon myself, I became compassionate and nurturing to halt my own mind from its assault on my innocence. I hadn't done anything wrong, but I believed that I had done something wrong.

Self-judgment had locked me in a cycle of resistance and struggle. All I observed in my life was more disappointment and personal dissatisfaction. Once I began releasing the story of being wrong or insufficient, believing that I was lacking something, that power of forgiveness transformed my energy field to a higher vibration, and I immediately began to attract more loving circumstances and wellbeing into my life.

I now feel the self-love and tenderness that I had been lacking for so long. I also don't hold myself hostage with self-judgment, which kept me from feeling the fullness of that passionate love. It is a beautiful and genuine relief to feel the warmth and tenderness that floods our hearts, when we give ourselves compassion and forgiveness.

Self-forgiveness for Shame and Guilt

For the practice of self-forgiveness to transform our lives, we can begin with those obvious experiences that bring up feelings of shame or guilt. These emotions are most often triggered by experiences common to all of us.

- **Career or Financial Failure**

"I must not have been good enough, so I was fired. Now I'll lose everything."

- **Divorce**

"I failed at marriage and tore my family apart. Now I'm alone."

- **Nontraditional Lifestyle Preferences**

"My sexual preference is unacceptable and wrong. I will never find true companionship and love."

- **Dysfunctional Family Dynamics**

"I am forever damaged by my family's abuse and neglect. I can't trust anyone I love."

- **Wounded Relationships**

"My mother put me in foster care because I was bad. No one is ever going to love me."

- **Addictive Behaviors**

"I can't seem to throw out anything. My hoarding is getting out of control because I can't manage my impulses."

- **Dissatisfaction with our Physical Appearance**

"Nobody wants me because I'm so fat. I look pathetic."

These dynamics give rise to a vibration of guilt and shame and ultimately, self-contempt, that is then harbored in our consciousness and contaminates our psyche, sometimes permanently, and on multiple levels. Not only will this powerful vibration attract more shame into our lives, but most people are never able to escape its unrelenting vengeance. Shame can stunt our natural ability to heal and grow by identifying with stories so intoxicatingly painful that most would rather never face such agony. Distractions, addictions, suppression and justification are the devices available to someone lost in shame and guilt. These are all subtle ways of judging and withholding love from ourselves, and they end up reinforcing our suffering.

However, the emotional states of shame and guilt are actually nothing more than vibrational energies that ignite "unconscious self-rejection. Unconscious, because it is inaccessible to the conscious mind but still affects our behavior and emotions. Self-rejection is the Inner Critic's voice that believes what we are feeling or experiencing is wrong and unacceptable. This voice is often faint, but can be shrewd and powerful, creating the sense within us that whatever feelings are present must be eradicated at all costs. This is the voice that tells us some version of the following: *I don't want to feel this way. It's wrong to feel this way. This is too difficult or painful to face. I've got to escape from this feeling somehow. When is this going to stop hurting? It's too much to bear. I want it to go away. I don't deserve to feel this way.*

This rejection of our emotional states (not accepting what is) is the activator of continual suffering, because it encumbers our consciousness with more avoidance and resistance. But if we stay with an emotional energy and allow it to be completely expressed, acknowledging and accepting it, without giving into any impulse to protect against it or control it, the sharpness of its sting begins to soften.

This softening enables us to feel the energetic resistance of the state of shame or guilt in the moment. It does so without adding more story of rejection, by encouraging us to accept what is. As we learn to accept our emotional states, we are able accept ourselves as we are. As we achieve that, we are no longer fractured into parts of us that feel good and acceptable, and the parts of us that feel bad, and unacceptable, that we reject. Uncomfortable thoughts and feelings are not wrong, nor do they need to be avoided. Once we begin to relate to these sensations as opportunities to Self-inquire, ("Who is suffering this shame?") instead of rejecting them, we begin to embrace our whole self with nurturing compassion and forgiveness. By consciously stripping away self condemnation, guilt and shame, we become more aware of what it is we need to forgive.

Forgiveness: Healing Our Wounds

As children, we take on and internalize the judgments and social values of our communities and caregivers. These include influence from our families, our race, our schools, and even our churches and religions. The power of this conditioning is to shape our self-esteem and identity. As children, we don't usually question the validity of our caretaker's judgment, and as a result, we are inclined to develop ideas about ourselves from the way other people in authority respond to us. Whether their responses actually had anything to do with us or not, we can be positively or negatively influenced by them. When we are negatively influenced, we begin to feel that we are "bad," or wrong, or somehow insufficient. These limiting beliefs soon become our deepest wounds, and if left to fester and grow, they will keep us unhappy and fearful. Self-forgiveness is the antidote to this type of suffering.

Throughout elementary school I was labeled a low performing student by the system. This meant that I was demonstrating either a lack of intelligence or a learning disability defined by the community that oversaw my educational progress. The school projected the judgment that I was a slow learner on me, and this had a significant impact on my psyche. I spent the balance of my academic years, and many subsequent years, struggling with my career under the notion that I was not up to par, and consequently, I learned to sell myself short, not taking risks that could have improved career outcomes, all to avoid the shame of failure. No matter what I had accomplished in life or how much I had achieved, I always discounted it, believing that if I had only been smart enough, I could have achieved so much more.

By embracing self-forgiveness, I have learned that who I am could never be a low performer or intellectually inept. I have always performed at the perfect level of my current awareness. Any thoughts of insufficiency in my abilities were transformed from unloving illusions or disparaging thoughts that I no longer have to bear, into a peaceful awareness that those thoughts are false, and who I am has always been enough.

It is essential that we become aware of moments when we have been triggered into feeling bad, wrong, not good enough, not smart enough, powerless or any variety of shameful emotions. By vigilantly guarding our attention in all situations, and becoming aware of unloving judgments we hold toward ourselves, we bring awareness, love, and self-forgiveness to those critical and judgmental thoughts and patterns.

By revisiting the place of the original wound in our "feeling memory," we discover that the negative ideas we adopted about ourselves are simply not TRUE. The truth is each one of us is unique, wonderful, and utterly lovable just as we are, and always have been.

When judgments and negative beliefs about ourselves arise in our thinking, we can examine our hearts and see the truth, remembering that the purity of our hearts and our deepest intentions were always to bring love to our self. By applying self-forgiveness and self-compassion we become aware of the untrue things that we were judged for as a child, and how we still might judge ourselves for them now.

Also, we can forgive ourselves for having feelings such as fear, anger, hurt, regret, disappointment, jealousy, envy, resentment and even hatred. These feelings can never be wrong or bad; they are just the direct result of our resistance to particular perceptions and experiences that happened to us in the past. Our emotions and negative feelings are a natural, healthy response to events. It is actually unhealthy to suppress, judge and condemn them, and ourselves, for having them.

Finally, judgment of ourselves for not fitting into an ideal of how we should be, is self-injurious, and must never be endured. When we vow to ourselves that we should be more like this person or that one or this ideal, or that one, we are acting contemptuously to our Self, and this behavior can never be tolerated. The being that each of us is—physically, mentally, emotionally and spiritually—in our wonderfully unique way, is nothing short of perfection, and a true gift to the world.

Ongoing Practice of Self-Forgiveness

The devotional practice of self-forgiveness is no quick fix or one-time healing episode, but a lifelong journey. We consciously choose to forgive our self again and again as new layers of resistance and judgment are unveiled for us to see and heal. When we benevolently care for ourselves, it means we are not allowing our minds to cling to the illusion of being wrong or deficient, especially when the criticism is directed at our Self.

There is a practice to staying vigilant and remembering to take the "best care" of ourselves and to nurture our own hearts. By taking the "best care" of our hearts, I mean:

- Paying close attention to our thoughts and how they make us feel.
- Remembering to catch ourselves in the same moment as when we are being critical, judgmental, or full of fear and worry.
- Acknowledging the stressful feeling or emotion we are experiencing.
- Forgiving ourselves for both believing in the story that evoked the original feelings, and the resistance we have to the emotion itself.

For example, let's say you take an important examination that will determine your professional certification, and you fail the test. You might feel rejection and just "not good enough." Instead of getting caught in a cycle of despair and self-loathing, try simply forgiving yourself. Remind yourself that this test could never determine your worthiness and remember that your feelings of disappointment and discouragement for failing the test are not wrong. This life-transforming forgiveness practice opens us to greater awareness about the truth of our original nature as innocent and is healing for our wounds. This allows and strengthens us in expressing our emotions without judgment.

This new loving way of relating to ourselves challenges what we have been taught, that negative thoughts are bad, toxic, and shameful, and will lower our vibration. We are also taught that in order to feel self assured and confident, we ought to banish negative thoughts from our lives. But resisting negative thoughts cannot be the path to freedom, and happiness does not depend on the number of negative thoughts we have; rather it depends on what we do with the ones we have.

By practicing self-forgiveness, we don't have to worry that we're having negative thoughts in the first place. Once we have forgiven our selves for believing self-condemning thoughts, we are instantaneously able to break free from the illusion of separation and return back to sanity.

Insanity implies doing the same thing over and over again and expecting different results. That is why believing that self-condemning and judgmental thoughts are a rational path to peace and freedom, is insane. Underneath the surface, many believe that if they shame or blame themselves enough they will be able to pay the debt for their perceived "wrong." But this is a form of self-punishment! Being able to separate our thoughts from our sense of self is one of the sanest things we can do. We are not our thoughts, and never have been. Any time we give our authentic identity or sense of Self over to a thought, we become insane.

Chapter 19

Forgiveness and Transformation Using STS

Transcending the Veil of Distortion

All of our thoughts and perceptions pass through the filters of our unique belief systems. These filters act as veils that can distort reality and can imprint negative thoughts into our psyches. Each is our personalized veil, the imprint of our childhood and adult wounds. These specific veils of distortion create the negativity we experience, not the negative thoughts.

Teachers of self-empowerment and the law of attraction believe that in order to create lasting positive change in our lives, we need to change the filter of our belief system. They believe that affirming a different belief system about ourselves will alter our thinking, but in truth we are the conscious awareness behind our thoughts, so "you" will never change. "You" can't—nor would you want to. You're perfect. There is no need to scrutinize those nasty critical thoughts or worry about them. They're just thoughts, not the truth of who you are. To have fewer worrisome thoughts, just stop listening to them! Forgive yourself for clinging to any illusion of "wrong" that may arise in consciousness.

Peace and contentment occur when our minds are quiet, and we remember that we don't have to believe our thoughts. And each time we remember to invoke this practice, and lovingly forgive ourselves by not forgetting who we are, we allow our awareness to align with the vast, unlimited energy field of light, love, compassion, healing and oneness.

Soul Transformation through Family Forgiveness

As an adult, I believed I had forgiven my parents for their insensitive abuse and the emotional neglect I experienced in my childhood. I realized their parenting style of harsh criticism and physical punishment was all they knew at the time. It couldn't have been so bad since I seemed to be highly functional and emotionally stable, or that's what I told myself. Although I still struggled sometimes with beliefs of unworthiness, I felt I couldn't blame them for that. But not surprisingly, I would still regularly recall childhood moments of pain and disappointment and harbor these wounds like battle scars. I would often tell painful stories of my childhood to my children and friends like they were from Grimm's Fairy Tales. I seemed to get some form of perverse pleasure from rehashing these old painful stories. I especially enjoyed describing my mother as a self-centered narcissist with the ability to reframe all of my childhood traumas without compassion for me, as someone who was only "all about her," and the trials she had to endure as my mother.

Even though I had forgiven my parents, the problem was that I still believed I should have received deeper nurturing and better care from them. I'm sure I forgave them because I believed it was the right thing to do. Conventional forgiveness allowed me to enjoy my parents as among the loving relationships of my life. But despite this pardon, thoughts of my family would still sometimes trigger pain and disappointment. I would often recall, and then relive, physical and emotional abuse from my parents, triggering a sense of being misunderstood and "not enough."

Nonetheless by all appearances, my life was successful. I had a circle of loving friends and family members plus a successful business; however I also never truly felt any of these good things. Instead of enjoying life, I spent most of my time feeling inadequate, always striving for more but never satisfied with anything. From all outward appearances, I was a man in control of his destiny, but I was constantly braced for disappointment or betrayal.

I was a convincing imposter, always appearing strong and confident so people never knew how insecure and fearful I was most of the time. As a big proponent of self-mastery, I encouraged "fake it until you make it," and always sported a convincing smile and positive attitude in spite of how I might have felt.

It was both exciting and repulsive to think about leadership. I enjoyed leading teams toward business success, but hated the disappointments of missing the goal, or in other words, not getting my way. When things didn't go my way, (and in business and they often didn't), I could become a big wounded child, angry, disillusioned and isolating myself from what I believed were the disappointed eyes of others. Any loss or let down felt like suffering, because it triggered my belief that I was, at core, still not good enough. Once I felt denied or overlooked I would brood and complain, sabotaging any opportunity to feel good, empowered, and loved.

The more business success I obtained, the more miserable I became. By the time I turned 50 years old I began to feel my life had gotten away from me. My business had grown too big, my family had gotten too burdensome and my health was failing. Lower back pain gradually became the center of all my suffering. This pain began to change the way that I saw myself. I had always been fit and strong, but I began to believe that I was disabled, making life choices based on how much pain I would be able to endure. The constant pain made me feel weak, incapable and exhausted. I felt as though my life was getting smaller and more restrictive. Just walking from my bed to the bathroom seemed to take a tremendous amount of effort at times. My pain had become so acute that I wouldn't travel unless I knew that I could get wheel chair service.

I tried every back-pain remedy. I heard about using experimental injections, but nothing would take away the tremendous pain. After two years of promises of cures from alternative medicine, I begrudgingly agreed to elective back surgery in hopes of alleviating pressure from my spine —but it only seemed to make things worse. After I had the surgery, I was diagnosed with what is known as "unsuccessful back surgery" because of the residual scar tissue from the incision. Having this surgery turned out to be my rock bottom. Afterwards, I experienced moments in which I wasn't sure I would ever walk without severe pain again.

Finally, my wife, Jocelyn, suggested that I try a very different kind of pain therapy that resolved resistance. This practice involved exploring childhood traumas that my body was still holding on to. This therapy proposed that our bodies are the repository of all our past unresolved and stored resistance, and until that is expressed or processed, our bodies will demonstrate dis-ease.

My wife was brave enough to speak to me from her intuitive heart. What she was sharing with me was something I didn't want to hear but I needed to. She told me that I frequently vented stories of my childhood pain, especially ones that represented my mother as the villain. Then she said something that threw me for a loop. She told me that if I could truly forgive my mother I would create a space for a healing. That the healing that I needed wasn't in my back but in my heart. Wow . . . what a wise woman!

I was completely baffled—first, that she would say such a ridiculous thing knowing how much back pain I suffered daily, and secondly, that it might actually be true. My mind didn't want to consider this farfetched idea, but something was telling me that it was right on.

I believed I had resolved all of my mother issues before she died four years prior. I loved her and missed her in my life. She was a remarkable woman with a strong sense of herself and command of her life. She was a survivor of abandonment and abuse herself. However, years after her death, I still recalled a certain emotional numbness I had experienced, about her passing-on.

Even so, on another level, to ascribe my current pain to unresolved mother issues was absurd to me. I wasn't about to rehash old childhood wounds to pursue a new kind of suffering. I was not interested in re-examining old perceptions of the painful inadequacies I believed I had during my childhood.

Still the idea of forgiveness kept arising in my consciousness until I discovered Colin Tipping's *Radical Forgiveness*. I learned that I didn't need to forgive my mother at all. What I needed was to overcome the "survivor" perspective of those childhood events by employing self-forgiveness and self-acceptance. My perceptions of my mother's criticisms and judgments—my unique *veil of distortion*—colored every aspect of who I believed myself to be. To heal those scars of distortion, I had to learn to love and forgive myself. I had to become aware of my self-condemnation, and then allow myself relief from deep feelings of inadequacy and "not-being-enough-ness."

Self-forgiveness has led me to discover an altered and much more aware perspective of the story of a sensitive boy, one who didn't understand that his mother may not have been properly equipped to raise a sensitive son. But with this new awareness, I was then able to see that she still loved him with all her heart.

I now understand that my mother operated from her own childhood pain and disappointments that negatively colored the way she viewed men in general. She was abandoned by her abusive father as a child, forcing her to drop out of high school at fifteen so that she could work to help care for her uneducated mother. My grandfather abruptly left his family, and then the family was forced to struggle, trying make ends meet, without him. As a teenager, my mother was performing extremely fatiguing physical labor, cleaning, ironing and folding hotel linen in a hot factory.

Once my parents got married they immediately began having children of their own. They decided that in order to make a better life for us that one of them would get an education. My father went back to school, got his Master's Degree in Education, and became a teacher in the Chicago public schools. Later on, when I was still in elementary school, my mother decided that it was her turn to get an education. She got her GED at 35 years old and then was driven to—not only finish college with honors—but also to procure a Master's Degree in Education.

By and by, as she struggled to both care for her children and pursue her own dream of a professional career, there would be times when all that would leave her feeling overextended and unsupported. These were the moments when she would lash out at her family both physically and verbally, complaining of being unappreciated. As her beloved son, I took on trying to protect her from this distress, doing everything I could to make things better for her, but it often seemed like my efforts were not enough. In retrospect, out of devotion to my mother and my sensitive nature, I inherited her wound as my own. In our Families Of Origin (FOO) are stories that we can spend our entire lives suffering over, that are not even our own.

But self-forgiveness has inspired me to become conscious of another story of who my mother may have been, one that better honors her memory, and also allows me to connect to her extraordinary and resilient heart. My mother was a strong and courageous woman who loved her family ferociously. She always fought for the best for us, never letting anyone get away with hurting or neglecting us. She taught me how to stand up for myself, but essentially, I believe, she showed me how to be generous and kind to others.

Forgiving myself for harboring unresolved resentment and disappointment became my pathway to enlightenment. I have since accepted that my family experience was the perfect setting for my own awakening. It fostered my tenderness and compassion for wounds of the heart and drove me to share my heart's awareness with students, colleagues, family, friends and other people, as my life's journey. By surviving my own childhood, I developed a passion for nurturing self esteem, motivating me toward a vision of peace and wholeness, one that I have found to be of service to others as well as to myself. Instead of just surviving, I began thriving and reaching out to those, like me, who were feeling stalled in their own personal development.

I am grateful that I now view my family and other intimate relationships in a whole new light. They are all my teachers, here to assist me in becoming aware of my resistances and my capacity for love. My back pain still flares up occasionally, but it is never severe and is always a blessing, for this pain has become a gentle reminder that as I forgive myself for perceived transgressions, I create space in consciousness for an aroused awareness, and the undeniable manifestation of miracles.

In conclusion, it is central to this practice of SoulTranSync that we transform our understanding of our lives, so that we can remember who we are, already perfect and always evolving. Then self-forgiveness offers us an expanded perspective of ourselves that is not condemning. In other words, soul transcendence requires releasing or clearing away that veil of distortion in favor of a viewpoint in which there is no right or wrong, good or bad. Only our limiting beliefs and perspectives define it as one or the other.

Summary of Part 3

Here is the summary of the **Three Core Elements of *Soul-TranSync*™** and its practices:

- **Acceptance** of the vulnerability of our own human heart, as "self" and its emotional nature.
- The gift of continuous **Gratitude** and appreciation for all aspects of life.
- The healing power of **Forgiveness**.

Each one of these principles is essential to spiritual alignment and can be incorporated into one easy practice that is simple to comprehend, stress-free to remember, and most vital of all, powerfully transformative.

In Part Four we will discuss what I offer as the most effective and complete practice for spiritual enlightenment. This practice synthesizes all of the principles discussed in Part Two into a concise and unpretentious daily devotion, that once rooted in our consciousness, will work on auto pilot to free us of our unhappiness. **Ho'oponopono** is a Hawaiian forgiveness practice that only requires the non-dual perspective of taking 100% responsibility for our entire lives. This includes all of our judgments, and the judgment of the entire Collective Consciousness.

The practice uses the mantra, "I love you, I'm sorry, please forgive me", and "thank you" to clear and clean away any old, stale memories.

The centerpiece of the Ho'oponopono practice is that only **you** exist as the SELF, that there is no "other." Everything else is only a perception or thought that can be dissolved, making room for Divine Inspiration.

With devoted practice of Ho'oponopono and its mantra, I continually uncovered new levels of my problematic "veil of distortion," and in turn, reprogrammed my consciousness with heartfelt awareness that continues to inspire a new way of Being.

PART FOUR

YOU ARE NOW READY TO SYNCHRONIZE TO THE SELF

The Ho'oponopono cleaning process allows direct contact with the divine wisdom, love and inspiration already within each of us. It is achieved when memories replaying as thoughts, fears, and judgments are transmuted to ZERO by Love. It is a state of being which enables us to lead inspired lives. And the only task in our life is the restoration of our Identities~our Minds~back to their original state of ZERO.[21] ~ Dr. Ihaleakala Hew Len Ph.D. t—

As an educator I have tried to be conscious of how the important concepts of this book are presented to ensure greatest comprehension. The progression of ideas in this book should cultivate in you an awakened awareness. It is for this reason I am only now sharing with you the approach to grasping this powerful practice that will immediately begin to transform and enhance your life. **You're now ready to Synchronize to the SELF.**

CHAPTER 20

SOULTRANSYNC AND HO'OPONOPONO

As you have progressed through the foundation of obtaining self-realization in P*art* One, and as I've introduced the tools for cultivating self-awareness *in Parts Two* and *Three*; you are now ready to understand the power and beauty of a simple tool for returning you home, back to the SELF or ZERO as it is called in the practice of Ho'*oponopono.*

Aside from its unusual Polynesian name and the difficulty in pronunciation, **Ho'oponopono** (*ho̲*-õ-pono-pono) has inspired a revolution in self-awareness that has spread throughout the planet. Traditionally described as an ancient Hawaiian healing process, *it* involv*es* forgiveness and reconciliation. Initially, Hawaiian mediators used t*his* technique as a tool to resolve both family and tribal disputes.

By breaking this unusual word down you learn that **Ho'o** is the Hawaiian version of a function word like the English particle, "to" and **ponopono** means many things such as "put in perfect order, correct, revise, amend, rectify, tidy up, or when put together, **Ho'oponopono** literally means, "to put in perfect order," or "to put to right."

Today **Ho'oponopono** is a healing practice grounded on the principles of assuming 100% responsibility for everything we see, hear, taste, touch or experience. Taking total responsibility supports the non-dual philosophy that everything exists only as a projection crafted from the human mind. 100% responsibility also includ*es* the idea that no one other tha*n* you even exists, that the seven billion people who reside on this planet are nothing more than seven billion individualized demonstrations of the same SELF, and that you are one with that consciousness. We might think of it this way: *there is only one of us here*!

In some way we are responsible for everything that appears in our life simply because it arises *in our life*. This isn't implying that we should feel guilty for all of the bad things that happen in the world, but rather, that we acknowledge the part we play in the events that happen to us. Recognizing the unconscious data or conditioning that plays itself out both in our own body-minds and those of all others.

The Ho'oponopono philosophy is that if we encounter violence, anger, misunderstanding and even suffering in others, there must be something in us that reflects these same tendencies. Furthermore the "external world" and the "inner world" of thoughts, memories and feelings are not separate; instead, they are seamlessly one.

From this unique point of view whatever we see in judgement outside of our bodies is also experienced *within us*. And because it appears or arises within us, we can clean and clear it by just working through the conditioned data allowing it to be released from the mind. Once useful data is released from the mind, we can stop arguing with reality and see that peace is naturally present, and find ourselves at home within it.

Ho'oponopono and 100% Responsibility

Ho'oponopono is based on the theory that anything that happens to you or anything that you perceive is entirely your responsibility. This includes the perceptions of the entire world where you live that is also your own creation, thus one hundred percent your responsibility, no exceptions.

If your wife is a tyrant and your children are bad students, it's your responsibility. And if there are wars and you feel bad because you are a pacifist? The war is your responsibility. You are aware of children around the world that are hungry, even starving. They too are your responsibility. You, as conscious awareness, are the creator of the world and are responsible for everything in it. What you are calling the world and perceive as the world is your creation, and only a projection of your own mind.

The practice teaches that accepting 100% responsibility doesn't mean it's your fault to bear, only that you are responsible for all your problematic thoughts and memories, and that by clearing those memories from your subconscious mind, you then resolve whatever or whoever it is that appears to you as a problem.

We possess the power to make our own choices in life. In essence, we create the world around us with the choices we make. You, and only you, hold any sort of power over your existence, and we need only imagine to open up new and positive possibilities. Once we accept this *total responsibility,* we gain a deeper awareness of how all experiences—good or bad—begin with ourselves.

CHAPTER 21

THE PRACTICE OF HO'OPONOPONO

The Ho'oponopono practice has three principal steps:

- Recognizing that whatever comes into your consciousness is 100% your creation and is the outcome of good and bad memories buried in your mind.
- Atoning for those memories through forgiveness to set you free.
- Closing with gratitude for awareness of SELF.

These steps are combined in a soulful four-part phrase or "mantra" designed to cultivate a new relationship with yourself. The practice of Ho'oponopono teaches that the mantra is addressing the Divine within us, but is responding to our human perceptions. These perceptions are more often than not the result of wounded imprints from our childhood. Distressing memories and other unsupportive thoughts of the collective mind are neutralized by simply repeating ***I love You, I'm sorry, Please forgive me, Thank You.*** The order in which the statements are made is not important, just allow the sequence of the mantra to arise through you organically.

Through time and practice you begin to realize that the mantra has infused itself into your consciousness as your new self-talk.

When before you may have easily slipped into a contentious reaction or responses to resistance, you now immediately align yourself back to love and forgiveness. The practice nurtures and heals our wounds both physically and mentally, releases memories from consciousness that cause resistance, and expands spacious awareness by continually reminding us of who we are.

In the book *Zero Limits*, Dr. Hew Len, the person most responsible in modern times for the widespread use of the mantra, makes it clear that this is not fast food, that the cleaning of memories requires both commitment and persistence, and in essence is a never-ending job. He emphasizes that as long as we are human we will have resistance and memories to clear.

Dr. Hew Len said "The only purpose in your life and mine is the restoration of our Identity - our Mind- back to its original state of VOID or ZERO; a state where one is free from the past, and immersed with Divine Intelligence and love." According to Dr. Hew Len, we can either respond from memory, or respond from inspiration.[22]

Ho'oponopono cleans DATA

ZERO is similar to the sky and the data is like the clouds that float across the sky. We are inclined to miss the sky because the clouds are so interesting and fascinating, so we lose track of zero because we are distracted and blinded by opinions, thoughts, memories, and the programming of our collective mind through socialization. So as clouds dissolve, the space of sky becomes more visible. Similarly, as we clean the data in our unconscious, we get a more spacious view of our true nature as the state of ZERO.

According to the Ho'oponopono philosophy, unconscious data is the main cause of our *suffering*. Our suffering is induced by all forms of resistant data, namely, clinging, aversion, and self-delusion, and by letting unloving and fearful data run us as we struggle and agonize in our lives. The practice extracts from consciousness this sticky data that causes our suffering, allowing us to evolve towards an awakened state where suffering ceases.

In an article on non-duality, "Words from the Wind; Philosophical Fragments," poet and philosopher Adam Pearson says that Ho'oponopono is paradoxical in its it's ability to be completely understood by the mind and the practical science of Ho'oponopono cannot be communicated except by using *the very unconscious data* that it is designed to clean. With the practice of Ho'oponopono, we never permanently abide at the state of zero, where all conditioning, opposites and conceptualizations are cut off. This soulful practice is best understood as a lifestyle of incessantly cleaning and clearing our way into ZERO, moment to moment, with our continuous data cleaning only revealing more memories to be cleaned.

Pearson goes on to explain that as we incorporate the work of clearing unconscious memories with the four-phrase mantra, we also can throw away the explanations of what Ho'oponopono is or how it works. In fact, we can say the four phrases cleaning the mind even of the explanations of the practice, in hopes that those thoughts too are erased along with the rest of the data that clogs up within us, conditioning our words and actions.

In the practice of Ho'oponopono Pearson calls this "abandoning the raft we used to get there . . . That it is the moon of zero that we are after, not the finger of explanations that point us to it. We use the words and concepts until we grasp the four phrases and how to use them; once we get that, we can drop the concepts and just live the practice."[23]

Living the practice means using the four phrases on whatever comes up in our experience, whether within our body-minds or within the world, as the primary form of the cleaning. Cleaning dissolves the unconscious blockages within us that keep us incoherent and resistant to change. All we need to know is how to do it, for it is the practice that matters the most. "Clean, clean, clean: understand what it is and then do it, constantly; this is the way of Ho'oponopono, the path home, to zero" says Pearson.

CHAPTER 22

HOW HO'OPONOPONO CLEANS WITH THE PHRASES: "I LOVE YOU, I'M SORRY, PLEASE FORGIVE ME, THANK YOU."

Now that you have a basic understanding of the way the practice works; we can begin to explore how you can relate to the **Ho'oponopono** mantra for maximum benefit. As we have discussed throughout this book, how we relate to ourselves is essential to spiritual alignment and enlightenment, but now you may see that this practice is a perfect tool for cultivating an awakened awareness. **But more simply stated when using this four-phrase mantra you are only ever speaking to yourselves about yourselves.** Although these four phrases are simple, easy-to-remember, and most importantly effective, they also tie you directly back to **Awareness** and the STS Core Elements already presented in Part Three of this book: **Acceptance, Forgiveness and Gratitude.** Breaking down the mantra into its parts will give you a context to its transformative power and a personal bond with the practice.

I Love You: This phrase is traditionally used as a proclamation of heartfelt devotion, affection and commitment to another. In this practice the statement is not object directed, but now turned around to the subject Self.

"I love you" has the effects of opening our hearts. It fosters acceptance, open-heartedness, love, caring, and empathy. And with frequent internal repetition of this phrase we begin to affirm the truth of our nature as Self. By saying "I love you" with genuine devotion in your heart, you proclaim you are one with the **source of all life**. This proclamation can also link your awareness to the process of nurturing your inner child with nonjudgmental, **unconditional love**, aligning your mind with healing and stasis.

Please Forgive Me: This statement is traditionally used when we believe—either known or unknown to us—that our actions have created some type of assault or offense to another. In this practice the statement is not object-directed either, but again turned around to the subject Self. By sincerely asking ourselves for forgiveness, we not only begin the process of correcting misaligned thinking but give ourselves permission to **clear** the slate of our own consciousness; erasing memories of unloving and unsupportive stories from our mind. Heartfelt forgiveness, especially to ourselves, opens the space for newly inspired perspectives to be revealed to us.

I'm Sorry: This statement traditionally acknowledges a deep regret or guilt for a wrong we may have committed, plus our willingness to atone for our actions. Even though the Self is incapable of committing an offense, our own psyches hold onto and often bear assaults on our innocence. "**I'm sorry**" encourages us to take responsibility and to own up to what we are doing rather than to deny or seek to avoid accountability.

When out of alignment the statement "I'm sorry" lets us atone to our consciousness, affirming that we are aware of our misalignment and are prepared to make corrections immediately. But reparation for our actions can only come when absolution simply washes away sin. With absolution comes the promise of rebirth, and the chance to escape the transgressions of our perceived mistakes.

Thank You. This phrase urges us to be grateful for life as it is presenting itself, and to become aware of the benefits that hide beneath the apparent misfortunes and troubles we encounter daily. With an "attitude of gratitude," we tend to be happier and feel more fulfilled as a result of this gracious outlook. Just saying this phrase of appreciation immediately encourages our minds to suppress our ego, and be presently aware of the blessings of our existence. This depth of intense appreciation releases our souls back to the source and the knowledge that the universe is all-encompassing and impersonal. By your repeating "thank you," we acknowledge that you are everything and everything is you—a whole, complete and universal.

The beauty of the **Ho'oponopono** mantra is its versatility. The phrases can be uttered anytime, anywhere, and in any order. And by practicing the four phrases, we begin to take ownership for our actions, our feelings, our thoughts, and everything we encounter, however unpleasant, violent, or suffering-instilled it may be.

These four simple phrases encourage us to be more mindful in our daily life, and pay closer attention to our internalized, conditioned thinking that has a tendency to run our lives without us even realizing it. This practice liberates our soul from the heavy burden of the ego's need for separation and control, gradually returning us back to our original state of *Zero*, where there are no mental complications, memory blockages, and thoughts to suffer in.

If the four phrases are expressed continually throughout your day in response to all internal resistance, your perceptions of reality soon become altered. You begin to see life in its perfection demonstrating in every moment. Peace of mind, trust in life, freedom and love become your default state of being. This new relationship with Self never diminishes but only grows in intensity in awakened awareness.

Ho'oponopono as a Consciousness Cleaning System

The following is a demonstration of how I used the four phrases to develop my own customized consciousness cleaning system. Through practice this technique has evolved into intimate and nurturing conversation that I have with my wounded or vulnerable states supporting a new internal dialog. This practice combined with my own awareness of Self has inspired peace of mind and untethered my soul from the demands of an unrelenting self-destructive ego, that allowed me to feel unworthy and unappreciated.

As I have awakened to my Self, I became aware that I had a tendency to judge and compare myself to others. Always wondering just how I measured up to my **imagined** ideal self, I would project my **imagined** deficiencies out onto others and then compare myself to them. I believed that I was either insufficient or superior to others in self-worth, abilities, attractiveness or talents. For example, I would believe "John is so talented. I wish I was as creative as he is," or "I have more experience than Bill. Why does he always get all the opportunities and attention?" While these compulsive and insane comparisons would made me feel temporarily better (ego aggrandizing), or worse (shameful and unworthy) about myself, they ultimately never made me any happier, peaceful or productive. My tendencies to compare myself to another was only a distracting behavior that kept me from seeing the truth of my dwindling self-esteem.

So when I was first introduced to the practice I was compelled to experiment with how to incorporate the four phases into a **consciousness cleaning system** that would clear my troubling beliefs. I was amazed with how the practice was transforming my perceptions, shifting my attention inwardly to Self, but I wanted also to use it as a tool to tackle the specific beliefs that caused suffering. So I chose to use it when my obsessive thoughts of comparison arose, integrating the four-phrase practice as my focus.

I first did an inventory of the occasions that I was triggered to judge others in compassion to myself, and soon realized that I would begin to feel isolated and vulnerable when I experienced a threat to my abilities. In the face of peril, I often responded like a deer in the headlights, my mind freezing up at the threat of failure. I could feel paralysis in my thinking and I would see no solutions to the problems I was facing. The difficulty was that this behavior would appear even though I was constantly pursuing innovative challenges or taking on new adventures.

Once I became aware of how my trigger was provoked, I was able to remember when to begin my cleaning work. Silently in my mind, I let the four phrases *(I love you, I'm sorry, please forgive me and thank you)* give rise to a natural flow of these words. In fact, I let the words arrive naturally without over-thinking or over-analyzing their order. I then began a dialog with myself that went like this:

I love you spacious awareness.

"**I'm sorry** for tormenting myself for the mistaken belief that I should compare myself to others by judging them as wrong or insufficient, knowing that only the wholeness and flawlessness of Self can exist.

I'm sorry for punishing myself when I believe I'm insufficient or less valuable than the people I compare myself to, knowing that only the Self exists and I am that.

Please forgive me for terrorizing myself by believing that an ideal more perfect Self exists that is not me.

Thank you for the awareness that any judgments of my value and worthiness are never meaningful, only thoughts in mind and I am not my mind. I am Self.

Thank you for showing me that when I compulsively strive to measure up to others and find myself either lacking or feeling better than them, this is only my inner child trying to feel good enough and longing to be loved.

Please forgive me for my lack of nurturing and compassion for my inner child. Denying his pain rather than accepting and embracing the vulnerability has not shown compassion or kindness to myself.

Please forgive me for misconstruing this contrived and delusional story of my value and worthiness as realities. The only realty that exists is the Self and I am that. **I love you**.

CHAPTER 23

ZERO IN HO'OPNOPONO

The practice of Ho'oponopono give us a compelling context to understanding the Self and grants us a new perspective on our existence. When we can look at the ego from the viewpoint of the ZERO, we gain an objective understanding of the nature of the ego and its claim to be our identity. ZERO introduces us to a new relationship with ourselves, giving us a distinction and preeminence over the psyche. This relationship allows us to disengage with the mind's functions, its preferences and tastes, its quests for personal growth and mastery, and its self-centered perspectives.

When we meet the awareness of Self at ZERO, we realize that we have previously assigned some of the Self's functions to the ego. In the state of ZERO we transfer the ego's functions to the Self, disempowering the ego from dictating our goals and accepting the Self's conviction of life in its perfection.

The Gifts of ZERO

In the ZERO state we gain many benefits from identification with the Self. These benefits include:

A deeper understanding of the mechanics of our thinking mind, free from the ego's distortions and fear of our shadows. In the ZERO state we are accepting all unwanted thoughts as nothing more than data to be erased.

A better managing of the mind's adaptability, including disturbing thoughts and stories, the ego's delusion of separation from Self, our unconscious resistance and the false mask or façade we present to the world representing our personality. With this fresh objectivity we gain greater awareness and flexibility and are no longer enslaved in our personal programming.

Control over the molestation of our minds, including the battles of the ego against the shadow, the unconscious mind and our sub personalities, for example the Worrier, the Critic, the Victim, and the Perfectionist; *all* sharing the ability to induce anxiety, and the negative dialogues that occur inside each one of us.

The ability to settle internal aggravations by not clinging to the ego's viewpoint. When our egos are balanced by the Self, we are less likely to provoke external battles by engaging ourselves with another *ego.* Love for all of humanity in its multitude of individual perspectives becomes our awakened viewpoint.

Better access to the unconscious mind's repressed memories, and the energy of its shadow content. This awareness prevent*s* us from unconsciously assuming the problematic qualities of our sub personalities. Causing worry about anything, even our desire to get our way, is a futile and impractic*al* waste of energy.

The Self doesn't discriminate or judge any of our personal human frailties; it just accepts them un-conditionally in love.

The freedom to accept and come to peace with all "opposite" traits, including the ones which are triggered from our wounded persona that we cast into the shadow. As Self there is no need for psychological repair or healing, all objects, especially the characteristics of the person, are evaluated as nothing special.

Finding clarity and objectivity regarding all of our personal traits and human perspectives with the ability to reevaluate our selections. Because our identity is invested in the holistic Self, we now have freedom to choose love over fear and to break our bondage to the ego's inflexible self-image.

Liberation from the imposed limits from the ego that break down the boundaries that hold our lives hostage. The Self is free of the ego's urgency, combativeness and emotional reactions. However, this detachment is not a cold withdrawal from life, but engages life more robustly without the weight of disappointment, judgment, and the need for control, instead accepting LIFE on its own terms.

By the realization that the Self has wisdom and power which are superior to that of the ego, we can sensibly and strategically submit to this greater entity, allowing the ego to receive direction from Self, contrary to the ego's short-sighted preferences.

With the Self's inclusive nature we are allowed a full spectrum of viewpoints from which to select our behaviors and identity, while embracing unique and individual points of view. The gift

> of individualism is now inspired with purpose, vitality and accuracy, instead of self-consciously projecting ourselves from the ego's ideas of self-enhancement and insufficiency.

In ZERO when we encounter the Self, we re-evaluate the limited perspective of ego as the center of identity, and its audacious claim to be our identity. What is revealed in the SELF is the ego's limited preferences and tastes, its quests for personal growth and accomplishment, and its self-centered perspectives.

CHAPTER 24

THE HISTORY OF HO'OPONOPONO

Like other mystical disciplines, the history of **Ho'oponopono** seems to indicate its roots sprouted from beliefs associated with similar ideologies. For example, indigenous populations on South Pacific islands such as Samoa, Tahiti, and Vanuatu have practiced transformative processes like **Ho'oponopono** since ancient times. Additionally, the Maoris of New Zealand regularly indulge in their own version of a "forgiveness" practice that includes many of **Ho'oponopono's** most recognizable attributes.

The earliest recorded reference to **Ho'oponopono** appeared in the Hawaiian newspaper, *Kuokoa*, in 1863. Mary Kawena Pukui documented her childhood experiences and observations of the late 1800s in a book she wrote in 1958 (Handy & Pukui). Pukui described **Ho'oponopono** as a practice to heal or "make right" severed family relationships. Prayer, confession, repentance, mutual restitution and forgiveness made up the bulk of these ancient traditional **Ho'oponopono** sessions.[24]

(Morrnah Simeona Picture)

Morrnah Simeona, a visionary Hawaiian healer, began to develop a streamlined style of_**Ho'oponopono**_in 1976. Influenced by her Christian education and her philosophical studies, she modernized **Ho'oponopono**_by merging the traditional Hawaiian practice with prayer to the Divine Creator as well as elements of karma and reincarnation.

Simeona's_update of_**Ho'oponopono** created a working relationship between the three parts of the self—unconscious, conscious and superconscious. Her methods have been researched and studied and continue to be documented in Hawaiian educational journals. Some of her former students, including Ramsay Taum and the renowned Dr. Ihaleakala Hew Len call her the modern mother of this world-famous healing practice.

(Dr. Ihaleakala Hew Len Picture)

The Famous Dr. Len Story and The Miraculous Story of Healing at the Hawaii State Hospital

Self-help marketing guru Joe Vitale was the first westerner to learn about a doctor in Hawaii who had cured an entire ward of criminally insane patients without ever meeting with them in person. The doctor was the legendary Ihaleakala Hew Len. As described in Joe Vitale and Dr. Hew Len's book *Zero Limits,* this monumental accomplishment was accomplished by harnessing the power of Ho'oponopono, he asserts that instead of attempting to interview and treat these patients, he chose to look within himself for the solution.

Dr. Hew Len believes in the premise that all problems we experience—such as the violence and chaos of a mental hospital for criminals—are simply the subconscious mind reliving past memories. He believed the only cure was to address the data or memories stored within his own subconscious. In a short time, the patients' destructive behaviors disappeared leading to some of them_a subsequent_release from the hospital.

The way the story is told in the book, *Zero Limits*, is that more than thirty years ago, in Hawaii, at the Hawaii State Hospital, there was a special ward, a clinic for the mentally ill criminals. The patients assigned to this ward were either suffering from very deep mental disorders, or they were under evaluation for mental competence to stand trial. They had committed murder, rape, kidnapping and other such crimes.

Testimonials from nurses and staff that worked there confess that the ward was in decaying, repulsive condition. Everyday patients would attack both members of the staff and other inmates. The staff was fearful and the turnover was frequent, resulting in chronic staff shortage. Because of security risks, inmates were never allowed outside to get fresh air because of the constant threat of aggressive violence.

Dr. Hew Len was the appointed clinical psychologist at the ward. The staff's impression was that he actually didn't seem to be doing anything in particular. He would come in everyday cheerfully smiling in a very natural, relaxed way. From time to time he would ask for the files of the inmates, but never tried to see the patients themselves. Witnesses say he just sat in his office and looked at their files. When staff showed interest in his practice, he would tell them about Ho'oponopono.

Quickly things started to change in the hospital. Patients that were never allowed to go outside started playing tennis with the staff. Other inmates became able to function without shackles or could respond favorably to less heavy pharmacological drugs. Many of them obtained permission to go outside unshackled, without causing trouble to the hospital's employees.

Over the four years of his tenure as the clinical director of inmate care, the atmosphere changed so much that the staff no longer avoided contact with the patients. Inmates once considered dangerous were gradually released. In the end, there remained only a couple of inmates that were relocated somewhere else and the clinic for the mentally insane criminals had to close.

When interviewing Dr. Hew Len on how he treated inmates to produce such spectacular results, he would say he didn't do anything other than looking at their files. He only attempted to heal himself by applying a traditional forgiveness practice from Hawaii called Ho'oponopono. In his own words: "I was simply healing the part of me that created them."

He explains that we would sit in his office and look at the patients' files. While examining their records he would feel empathy for them, identifying with their diagnosis and histories. Then he would begin the healing on himself, taking full responsibility for what was going on with a given patient. Dr. Hew Len insists that this was how these inmates got better; that it was himself who needed the treatment as he called clearing and cleaning, not the patients.

CHAPTER 25

MY STORY OF SOUL TRANSCENDENCE WITH HO'OPONOPONO

Throughout my life, I have now realized that my disappointments and pain have only prepared me to do great things and inspire love in others. In those moments I was rarely able to see the blessings and miracles that were right in front of me. I chose to face myself in a new way, healing old wounds and reemerging as the Self through the practice of Ho'oponopono.

At forty years old I was gifted with a vision that at that time I believed was revealing to me my true destiny. I had never been satisfied in my corporate career, feeling that my life had a more important calling than making money for cooperate giants and earning a paycheck from it.

I always imagined a life of service to the world, where I was inspiring empowerment and self-reliance to less advantaged communities. Even in college I was passionate about community empowerment, actually interning during the 70's at a nonprofit Community Development Corporation in Boston. I believed this work was the noblest, most honorable career I could have. At that time I had a very strong passion for creating a new world that would include opportunities that didn't leave anyone out.

So once I graduated from college my first objective was to work in some form of social services. The problem was that there were no jobs that I was qualified for at the time. Though disappointed, I settle for climbing the corporate ladder and gave up my dream of inspiring lives.

In the late 90's I was introduced to a brand-new concept at the time called charter schools. Charter school legislation in Florida had just been passed, and no one really understood what these schools were, but the objective of the law was to privatize public education to empower community accountability. This was at least its initial intent. It later evolved into another opportunity for corporate profits once the industry was ripe for industrialization. This was not my objective. I just wanted to make change in people's lives.

Because I believed that my early school years had been harsh and un-supporting, I dreamed of designing schools that inspired poor lower-performing students to succeed, feel nurtured, and inspired. Statistically, poor minority students had a soaring high school dropout rate, with black boys' third grade test scores forecasting future prison populations. I believed that all children could be successful students in a supportive environment, and that no child should ever feel like a failure as I did in my early school years.

So in 1997, under great fanfare and much scrutiny, I was approved to open Smart School Charter Middle, the first charter middle school in Florida. As a result of my lack of educational experience, and limited financial resources, short of raising two outspoken daughters, this process turned out to be the greatest challenge of my life.

That year, every step of the way, I faced major obstacles, from finding an appropriate site for a middle school to funding the startup. But for some reason no matter how insurmountable the obstacles were, I was blessed with solutions and resources to proceed with opening my charter school on time that next year.

Even though I had no money for books and supplies, and no experience at running a school, nor a location to house the students, companies who were excited about my success made donations to the cause. I felt blessed and favored because I was now perusing a noble passion.

There was enormous support from the parents, business, and political leaders in the community. They were thrilled that I was providing an alternative to their local failing schools. They would praise me for my passion and vision in the community.

Although I was inspired with passion for the cause, I was also terrified of failure. And although I was faithful in my pursuit, I felt overwhelmed and suffered from anxiety and panic most of that year. My new charter school received both a controversial and inspiring weekly story in the local press that year. People I approached for support or assistance had two reactions, they would be either excited about my success or resentful that I was taking financial resources away from the local school systems, to squander them away in this charter school experiment.

Despite almost impossible obstacles, I was able to get the school open that first year on time. Even though this was a real accomplishment, opening the school that year turned out to be the easy part.

In that first school cycle, just about everything that could go wrong, did go wrong. The white Harvard graduate principal that I hired quickly turned out to be a bust. Although he looked great on paper, he was actually intimidated and afraid of the black students that had enrolled in my school. Within the first month he had decided that the students' behaviors were so bad that we needed to hire more security guards to police the campus. Also, many of the teachers he hired were mostly unskilled new teachers with no experience in managing a classroom or maintaining discipline.

By the second month the school had turned into a combat zone, with fights breaking out hourly, bathrooms vandalized daily, and food fights in the cafeteria. Although I was way over my head, I knew that if the school was to survive the year I would have to step in and take back the reigns of control from this unqualified, inappropriate leadership I had put in place. So I did.

The first thing I had to do was fire the Principal and assume the role of Acting Principal until I was able to hire a new one. I knew nothing about running a school, so to hold me over until I found new leadership, I depended on advice and direction from principals and administrators from other nearby district schools. Even though these seasoned educators were unsure about me, charter schools, and my complete lack of experience, some of them turned out to be angels, offering all they could to help me through this vulnerable and terrifying moment.

I discovered a young talented Assistant Principal named Dwight who demonstrated passion for educating black students. I had discovered that passion for the heart and mind of the students in my school was most important to me, especially since my last principal had no interest in educating black children without an army of police. I asked Dwight if he would consider leaving his school districts job to assume leadership of my untested, and now struggling, new charter school. You can imagine that he was a little tentative to leave the security of the district school and risk his reputation on an unproven venture. But I believed this young man was special; I let him know if he accepted this position, I would give him full authority to run the school his way. I actually had nothing to lose since I certainly didn't know what I was doing, and desperately needed help fast. We agreed to terms of employment except he was unable to start working for me until after the Christmas break.

So for two months that autumn I actually ran this two hundred student charter school with no professional help on my staff. Even though I had no idea what I was doing, I somehow stabilized, and even revitalized, the school culture. And what the universe provided to me for help was a family therapist who had just walked into my school one afternoon, and a hardworking loyal security guard. With this heartfelt but untrained team, we were able to develop a totally transformed school culture.

During my short reign as Acting Principal I did everything I could to connect with the students. As a corporate executive, I knew how to rally a team and engage the students in a vision for their new school. I created teams, offering awards for both academic and behavior competitions. Even though I have never been athletic or even participated in organized sports, I created leagues and even coached basketball after school. The students of Smart School loved that. Most of them would have never had a chance to play on a team at another middle school. But at Smart School all were welcome.

However, what changed my life that year was meeting the first eighth grade class. They were a ragtag group of fifteen-year-olds that had failed, or were struggling in traditional district middle schools. Many of them had become disillusioned with school, and most were initially very skeptical that Smart School would be any better. That first year we didn't have any of the programs and resources that they were used to, but their parents believed that we were their last hope.

To reinvigorate the school culture, I was determined to get the eighth graders engaged in the school, believing that the sixth and seventh graders would then follow, and it worked. I felt honored that these families had chosen to stick with the school after our chaotic launch.

I developed a powerful personal bond with those eighth-grade students. I saw myself in the heart of each one of them. Many of them, like myself, had struggles in school, either from having been bullied, ignored, or just unsupported. It was important to me to give them a voice, and empower them to participate in turning the school around.

By Christmas we had made major changes in the school culture. Fighting and vandalism had stopped. Even the teachers were calmer and more productive. When I turned over the school to

Dwight that January he was able to immediately put into place structure, organization, and discipline, making the school not only functional but high performing.

Dwight saw that the students had developed a special affinity to me. We had bonded during those transitional two months, and I wasn't sure how to back off. Whenever the eight graders were discontent with Dwight, even though they liked him a lot, they would ask that I fire him and take back the school. Even though I would never consider it, it touched me so that they really liked and trusted me, especially since I had no idea what I was doing.

Although the balance of the school had its ups and downs, my young talented principal turned everything around. By June we had created something really special at Smart School. We had a waiting list of students for the next school year and were recognized as the preferred middle school in the community.

At the end of that school year we decided to put on a traditional eighth grade graduation. This was my opportunity to recognize all of the heroes that had helped us make it through, but most important it was my chance to say goodbye to a ragtag bunch of eighth graders that had changed my life. They were so proud and grateful to have been part of our inaugural year. A lot of them stayed in touch with me during their high school years. And the result has been that even twenty years later I'm still mentoring, supporting and loving many of these now young adults from the graduating class of 1998.

Over the sixteen years of operating schools, I managed two middle and two high schools, serving thousands of students and families.

Dwight was by my side most of those years. He obtained his doctorate in education leadership and became a recognized advocate and expert in developing successful urban schools.

But as for me, now in my mid-fifties, I was burning out and had become disenchanted with the bureaucracy and tremendous responsibility of managing the schools. I had reached a point where my identity of community leader and education visionary had become too heavy for me to bear. My work as a community visionary and revolutionary was now relegated to managing budgets and solving employee problems, and my attitude of passion and enthusiasm for the community had deteriorated into resentment. All I could see at that time was more problems and pain, and it wasn't going to get any easier. I was both emotionally and physically exhausted and just wanted out.

During the last few year of managing the charter schools I had discovered Ho'oponopono, and the practice had begun to shift my intentions from saving the community to inspiring the world. It was a gradual process but I was now getting a glimpse of what my true purpose was, that it was bigger than my mind could conceive and the open heart of my inner child was relating to this new awareness.

I realized that my true identity could never be the stories of my wounded perspectives. My mind had created these stories only as a framework to inspire my soul evolution. I began seeing that every challenge and emotional resistance I had experienced in life were simply opportunities to love. This practice was altering my attention and even reconstituting the way my mind worked. Love, gratitude, and forgiveness for myself became my objectives, and learning how to tenderly nurture myself became my new greatest challenge. This was the Soul Synchronization my heart had been calling for so long.

But beginnings and endings are often the most difficult. All of the emotional resistance I faced in launching my first charter school was nothing compared to the suffering I had to endure once I choose to retire from the schools.

In order for my life to have this new chapter and freedom, I believed that I needed to completely disengage from the identity that I had created as Mr. Miller. This meant disassembling all of my charter schools, including all the other affiliated community ventures I had started throughout the years.

I was aware that the parents, my teachers, and the community didn't understand why I was doing this. What they saw was that I was thoughtlessly taking away the schools that had become important institutions in the community for over 15 years. Families that had supported our schools over the years saw us as a community tradition, a safe and nurturing environment for their children to have academic success. But what hurt the most was that the children, whom I loved and had created the schools for, were furious with me. They believed that I was selfishly taking their beloved charter schools from them.

On the final day of school I decided to sit in a classroom with high school students. I realized that this was going to be my last opportunity to be among students and I wanted to feel their energy for one last time. But what I wasn't aware of was just how hard this loss was on them. I witnessed their anger, tears and resentment for me, but I also understood that they too needed closure.

CHAPTER 26

LOVING MYSELF

For six months after retiring I allowed myself to mourn the end of an identity, a hero's identity that was built out of my passion to inspire and empower others, but at the same time I struggled with a shadow of unworthiness. It was at this moment I realized that life was once again asking me if I was willing to heal these wounds. It was this opportunity to grow that instigated my dark night of the soul.

During this moment I allowed myself to disconnect from all of my family, friends and business associates. I didn't want to explain or even justify my feeling of intense pain and isolation to anyone. My heart was breaking, and I just wasn't capable of feeling anything outside of grief, loneliness and failure.

My anguish at that time was disappointment. I believed that my decision had let everyone down, including myself. I had turned my back on a thriving and beloved community resource created to inspire lives, and I wasn't even sure why I did it. Although I had always wanted to make a positive difference in people's lives, I had now thrown it all away because it seemed to be getting too hard and I wasn't even happy. Maybe I wasn't a hero at all, just an opportunist that bailed once the business got too difficult.

I was very aware that I was stuck in a story of unworthiness that had infected my entire outlook. I wasn't able to see any part of my life as hopeful. Everything in my life seemed too difficult for me.

I also was lamenting some of the choices I had made that kept me stuck in always trying to substantiate my worthiness. I had been a pioneer in the charter school industry, but while other new charter school management companies were building school districts around the country, I was still struggling with managing and maintaining my original four community schools. The industry seemed to be leaving me behind struggling with the challenges and disappointments of holding together an impoverished and depressed community. I started believing that it was my destiny to bear all of the wounds of the children and families that I was serving.

For a while all I was able to do was sit in darkness and suffer in seclusion. I felt numb inside, and for months I could barely eat or sleep. My wife had just lost her father and was also feeling great despair at that time. Staying strong and supportive for each other when vulnerable had been the pattern of our relationship over the years, but at this time neither one of us had much strength to comfort the other in this darkness, although our love and devotion to one another was still strong.

Even in experiencing this dark place of pain, I was aware that it contained gifts of healing. So I avoided my tendency to jump into a new projects or distractions, and instead decided to see the pain as an opportunity to face all the shadows of myself. I wasn't willing to rush through my process of getting over this, instead I accepted each painful moment as it was presented to me.

Eventually I found the strength to begin a new dialog with myself. Meditative inquiry and the Ho'oponopono practice became sacred sustenance, and my new way back to Self. Although my mind was struggling with all of its shadow identities, instinct was telling me it was now time to begin to nurture my unattended wounded child. It was in this dark place that I began to use this meditation practice to cultivate a new relationship with my inner child.

I knew that the subconscious mind is where all our memories are stored, and in deep meditation this mind can be both opened to new suggestions, but also reveal and release old trauma.

When I first began practicing I felt great resistance battling my ego. The four phrases not only didn't feel right, but actually inspired more anxiety. My mind just wasn't able to profess love for myself through all the darkness that I was feeling, so I chose instead to reach out to my inner child who had heard all my stories of unworthiness. I believed that in my innocence I was perfect, whole, and complete and that if I reengaged with the wounded child within me, I might be able to reintroduce myself to that innocence.

I found a kindergarten class picture of myself at five years old. I realized that although that little boy was sensitive, he was also smart, creative, and adventurous. I placed the picture as my screen saver on my cell phone so that I could have him with me at all times, even in meditation. Looking at the sweet, kind face of my childhood ignited compassion and a desire to nurture the innocence that had been wounded from years of my own desertion and neglect.

On first contact with my inner child I felt a sense of hesitation, even anxiety from that sensitive boy. As a child I recalled sometimes feeling disregarded by teachers and also my parents. This feeling of neglect and loneliness triggered my insecurity, often exiling me to behaviors of isolation. Even now as an adult whenever my self-esteem is threatened, I can revert back to that wounded child, afraid to face those feelings, choosing to hide my shame and self-doubt about my self-perception of weakness.

But it was easy to say *I love you* to that boy. I knew how badly he had wanted acceptance and to be thought of as be "good enough." In meditation I would visualize him sitting on my lap allowing me to comfort him. I would hold him close to me and say *Please forgive me for my lack of acknowledgement of your tender and sweet heart. I'm sorry if I have ever been intolerant of your emotional vulnerability, knowing that you were only trying to get my attention. Thank you for trusting me to care for you now.*

Every day for weeks I would spend time in meditation reconnecting with my inner child. After some time I began to feel our relationship started to evolve. Cultivated feelings of tenderness and warmth were now receiving nurture, so my inner child was now responding back to me with joy and enthusiasm. I realized that essential to my own self-esteem was how passionately I protected, nurtured, and cared for the vulnerability of the inner wounded child within me.

For a long time that child had gone unrecognized, and whenever acknowledged, was condemned as weak and emotional. I was intolerant of these emotions and rarely willing to accept any feelings of helplessness that would arise in me when vulnerable. Like many men I believed weakness and helplessness was wrong, and feeling that way also made me wrong. By not recognizing the sensitivity and tenderness of my wounded child, I had shut down my heart. Once my heart was properly and sufficiency closed everything seemed difficult and pointless. I had been feeling overwrought and uninspired for a long time. I no longer could tolerate the feeling of numbness that had taken over my heart through the years. I wanted to feel passion and enthusiasm again, and I knew that connecting with my inner child was the only way back to my heart.

In this new relationship with myself I was now inspired to reexamine my life, and see the perfection of how life had unfolded for me. With the practice of Ho'oponopono memories began to reveal to me that the true character of my inner child was uniquely qualified for the challenges and responsibilities that I would face in life. And although my inner child was strong and imaginative, he was also sensitive and needed nurturing and acknowledgment.

The problem was that I had generously invested in stories of lack and limitation, and unknowingly become accustomed to telling my child about my inadequacies and shortcomings. The pay-off for my investment was some perverse sense of humility or modesty. I realized now that by constantly putting myself down I was destroying my self-esteem or self-confidence. This included the words I said out loud in addition to my internal self-talk. Negative words as well as my negative thoughts had distorted my perceptions, and I needed to forgive myself for years of these assaults. Self-awareness required that I pay better attention to these habitual unloving thoughts, then stop telling my child things like I wasn't smart or talented enough. This self-effacing, false humility was my way of lowering expectation for failure, but it also cultivated hopelessness and despair in my child.

In my meditation I began telling my child how brilliant, worthy, and capable he was. Although I had been reluctant at sharing this with my child, I promised to never overlook him again. Somehow this nurturing ignited childhood memories of glory and accomplishment that had been drowned out or suppressed by years of reinforced negative self-talk. It seems that all my inner child really needed was nurturing and compassion to begin revealing to me a whole new reality about my life that had been obstructed by memories.

This new relationship began to reveal to me that even as a child I was a strong creative leader, gifted at inspiring others to follow my vision. Actually, The Green Leaf Club that I founded when I was eight-years-old was my first successful business venture. Leading a team of kids to perform that evening had somehow imprinted my consciousness, and later in life gave me the authority and courage to become a leader in the charter school movement.

I started to remember how audacious I was as a child for taking on important duties that others couldn't have handled, and maybe that's why my parents put so much responsibility on me. I could now recall that as a child I had always been recognized and appreciated for my sense of responsibility and follow-through, like on that definitive Christmas morning when I was eleven-years-old. My parents counted on me to get important things done properly and their neglect at remembering my gift turned out to be the greatest gift to myself, since it empowered me to become conscious of the importance of also having my own needs met.

Even my teachers selecting me to play the lead role of the king in the middle school production of "The King and I" had imprinted leadership and responsibility in my young psyche. And playing this strong heroic character whose ultimate concern was doing the right thing for the people he was responsible for was etched into my heart, changing my life forever. My courageous child learned not to allow fear of failure to dissuade him from conquering whatever his brave heart was called upon to take on.

So as an adult this *can-do* attitude gave me the wherewithal to go after big impossible dreams with confidence and passion, eventually taking on the heroic intention of uplifting a struggling community. Cultivated by my desire to be of service to the world and heal broken hearts, my attitude was caring for these thousands of children of Smart School that had been my destiny, and I finally could see that it was my own wounds that were healing. By enduring all of the challenges and obstacles of running this community school, I faced all of my shadows of unworthiness, and learned the truth about myself.

As I transformed my relationship with my inner child, a new awareness of the wholeness of SELF emerged, igniting a soulful passion for life. Love and forgiveness for myself eventually opened a new gateway through my heart, connecting me to the tenderness and vulnerability in the hearts of all men and woman. The passion to share with others how to genuinely care for their own tender hearts emerged out of my own darkness.

Sharing the practice of SoulTranSync with the world manifested out of desire to liberate my old unloving memories or stories into spacious awareness, I forgave myself for believing them in the first place, letting them grow so heavy on my psyche. I accepted my true nature as Self, never insufficient, only whole, complete and perfect as I AM and expressed *Gratitude* for the awareness that life in its perfection is unfolding for my good, always guiding me back into the passions of my heart.

My own soul transcendence was born out of the awareness that the incriminating thoughts in our minds and bodies are not always real, and that all our suffering is the result of believing that they are. SoulTranSync is the practice of remembering this truth, accepting our nature as the SELF, forgiving ourselves for believing all illusions, but also offering genuine gratitude for our life as it revealed to us.

This was the sacred medicine I took to transcend my suffering and to learn to live life from true inspiration and heartfelt passion. It is my greatest hope that you consider this remedy as your path to freedom. The downloadable workbook is free, and is a perfect companion tool to assist you in your journey of awakening.

I love you, I'm sorry, Please forgive me and Thank you.

CHAPTER 27

LET'S WRITE THIS ONE TOGETHER

I am honored that you have taken the time to read this soulful book. I wrote Soul Power from an overflowing heart of love and compassion, but in the course of writing this book I personally experienced a life altering cathartic journey. I am now inspired to share with other soul partners my journey of exploring vulnerabilities and innocence, and how I learned to align in awareness of a new way of BEING.

Although foremost this new relationship explores identity, (who am I) and the truth of our own nature, I also share how by deconstructing our ego identities we cultivate Self-love, Self-acceptance Self-gratitude and most overlooked Self-forgiveness.

This peace, love and freedom that our hearts are seeking are here with us NOW and always. But even as this enlightened state is our truth, it often is veiled by our compulsive wanting and desiring of ego. Only in spacious awareness are we able to remember our true nature, and drop all our stories of separation.

The practice of Ho'oponopono is a powerful tool for revealing truth. It does this by clearing burdensome memories that surface in mind; releasing them back to spacious awareness or what the practice calls Zero. The practice teaches that we must first take 100% responsibility for everything that shows up in consciousness. There is no blame, shame or guilt because the practice affirms that only God exists, and that all human perceptions are nothing but illusions.

As a collective we have just recently evolved in human conciseness out of the age of reason and understanding, to the new age of heart and compassion. Especially right now the world needs practical, simple but powerful tools like Ho'oponopono to evolve our hearts and create the space in consciousness for world peace and abundance of resources. I'm convinced that only a Heart Revolution will challenge the old order of mind, and usher in without restraint a new consciousness, one that promotes empathy, kindness, sensitivity and global concern.

We now need leaders that are passionate about the future of our planet to spread the word of this new order. Leaders who will modify their relationship with themselves in love, and share with others the simple mantra of "I love you. I'm sorry, please forgive me, thank you.

This is your invitation to become a writer of our next chapter. If you enjoyed this book and gained even a few insights that will help you be different, think differently, and lead differently, please share them with others. Share what you have learned with your family and friends, and any others who you believe could benefit from this book, and then make it known to others. These are the strategies to starting a heart revolution.

Also I invite you to visit my website, www.soultransync.com, to sign up for my newsletter and to join the STS Community. You will also be able to download a free STS meditation.

Our website will announce all STS webinars, workshops, and seminars centered in Self Love and cultivating greater awareness. The more connected we become, the more we will be able to share ideas, support each other, and create accountability for the things we seek to achieve. Collectively, not only can we help each other to grow and learn, we can also make a difference and have a positive impact in the lives of so many and be of service to countless others too! Come join us!

- **Write a book review on Amazon** (www.amazon.com). Your impressions and takeaways matter. I'm looking forward to being your reader now and learning more about the *impact* this book had on you, and what you gained from reading **Uncovering and Embracing Soul Power**
- **Keep building our impact with the e-learning program.** If you find yourself inspired to the point of taking that next important step in the SoulTranSync practice, I have good news for you. I have created a free workbook that supports the practices of STS. Here is a link www.soultransync.com/workbook to download the content. This workbook will support you in using the STS practice in your daily life, and assist you in developing a deeper, more compassionate relationship with yourself.

- **Stay in touch.** Reach out to me with questions or comments about the book. Please feel free to connect with SoulTranSync via Facebook and Instagram or email me at soultransync@gmail.com

Let the diversity of human experiences transform who you are, as you transform the world we all live in.

Thank you,

Edward

Bibliography

[1]Tolle, E. (2009). A quote from A New Earth. Retrieved April 7, 2020, from https://www.goodreads.com/quotes/6483962-the-primary-cause-of-unhappiness-is-never-the-situation-but

[2]Zukav,G. (2007). The Seat of the Soul. Retrieved April 7, 2020, from https://worldbusiness.org/fellows/gary-zukav/

[3]Chopra, D. (2018, December 13). The Classic Pamela Positive: "The Soul Is the Core of Your Being."- Deepak Chopra. Retrieved April 7, 2020, from https://pamelahawley.wordpress.com/2018/12/13/the-classic-pamela-positive-the-soul-is-the-core-of-your-being-deepak-chopra-2/

[4]Papiji. (2017, April 29). 25 quotes from Papiji. Retrieved April 7, 2020, from http://universoulawakening.com/25-quotes-from-papaji/

[5]Nim. (2014, April 9). Quote Investigator, We See Them As We Are. Retrieved April 7, 2020, from https://quoteinvestigator.com/2014/03/09/as-we-are/

[6]Katie,B. (2020). Goodreads. Retrieved April 7, 2020, from https://www.goodreads.com/quotes/9501106-i-discovered-that-when-i-believed-my-thoughts-i-suffered

[7]Rowling,J. (2020). Goodreads. Retrieved April 7, 2020, from https://www.goodreads.com/quotes/303377-always-the-innocent-are-the-first-victims-so-it-has

[8]Swoboda,K . (2020). Your Courageous Life. Retrieved April 7, 2020, from https://www.yourcourageouslife.com/silencing-the-inner-critic/

[9]King,D. (2015, January 1). THE HEART CHAKRA: THE CENTER OF YOUR BEING. Retrieved April 7, 2020, from https://dcbo rahking.com/the-heart-chakra-the-center-of-your-being/

[10]Frawley,D. (2000). *Vedantic Meditation* (Electronic Edition ISBN 978-58394-956-6 ed., Vol. 3.1 page 12). Berkley, California: North Atlantic Books.

[11]Adyashanti. (n.d.). The Impact of Awakening. Retrieved April 7, 2020, from https://www.facebook.com/adyashanti.org/posts/go-to-the-pure-i-am-not-i-am-this-or-i-am-that-but-simply-i-am-then-throw-out-th/506425149722659/

[12]Singer,M. (2016, January 13). Quotes from The Untethered Soul by Michael A. Singer. Retrieved April 7, 2020, from https://isaiahlim.wordpress.com/2016/01/13/quotes-from-the-untethered-soul-by-michael-a-singer/

[13]Mooji. "20 Powerful Quotes by Mooji That Will Help You Understand His Key Ideas." *Ideapod*, 9 July 2019, ideapod.com/20-powerful-quotes-by-mooji-that-will-help-you-understand-his-key-ideas/.

[14]Tolle, E. (2016, December 24). 75 enlightening Eckhart Tolle quotes that will blow your mind. Retrieved April 7, 2020, from https://ideapod.com/50-enlightening-eckhart-tolle-quotes-that-will-blow-your-mind/

[15]Oliver, M. (2015). The Summer Day. Retrieved April 7, 2020, from https://womenintheworld.com/2019/01/18/poet-mary-oliver-tell-me-what-is-it-you-plan-to-do-with-your-one-wild-and-precious-life/

[16]Tolle, E. "TMM Book Review #2 - The Power of Now - Eckhart Tolle." *The Mental Movement*, 1 Apr. 2015, www.thementalmovement.com/2015/04/01/tmm-book-review-2-the-power-of-now-eckhart-tolle/.

[17]Maharaj, N. (Ed.). (2008). I AM THAT. In *I AM THAT* (Sudhakar S. Dikshit ed., Vol. one, pp. 14–15). Durham, North Carolina: Acorn Press.

[18]Eckhart, M. “Meister Eckhart Quotes.” *BrainyQuote*, Xplore, www.brainyquote.com/quotes/meister_eckhart_149158.

[19]Sahn, S. (n.d.). Kwan Um Zen. Retrieved April 7, 2020, from https://www.ebslr.org/kwan-um-zen

ZERO-WISE Our Mission Statement. (2018, April 7). Retrieved April 7, 2020, from https://www.zero-wise.com/mission-statement/

[20]Emerson, R. (2012, November 21). Cultivate the habit of being grateful for every good thing that comes to you. Retrieved April 7, 2020, from https://omarkiam.wordpress.com/2012/11/21/cultivate-the-habit-of-being-grateful-for-every-good-thing-that-comes-to-you/

[21]Montenegro, R. (2011, March 27). How Dr. Hew Len healed a ward of mentally ill criminals with Ho’oponopono. Retrieved April 7, 2020, from https://hubpages.com/religion-philosophy/How-Dr-Hew-Len-healed-a-ward-of-mentally-ill-criminals-with-Hooponopono

[22]Hew Lin, I. (2007, January 2). 528Heals.com. Retrieved April 7, 2020, from https://www.528heals.com/hooponopono

[23]Pearson, A. (n.d.). The Twin Paradoxes of Hooponopono. Retrieved April 7, 2020, from https://philosophadam.wordpress.com/2012/09/16/the-twin-paradoxes-of-hooponopono/

[24]Pukui. “Ho’oponopono, ‘to Make Right’: Hawaiian Conflict Resolution and Metaphor in the Construction of a Family Therapy - PDF Free Download.” Slideheaven.com, slideheaven.com/hooponopono-to-make-right-hawaiian-conflict-resolution-and-metaphor-in-the-const.html.

ACKNOWLEDGMENT

I would be remiss without acknowledging the most significant influencers and inspirations in my personal soul journey. My mother Ida as teacher and muse, encouraged me to a life of introspection and soul searching, fostering an inquisitive open mind. Later in search for answers to understanding my Self, I discovered important awareness expanding spiritual guides. These great teachers include Krishnamurti, Echkart Tolle, Brene Brown, Tara Brach, Adyashanti, Rupert Spira, Charles Geddes and, most importantly, the pointing of Mooji, who inspired me to awaken to my natural true Self.

ABOUT THE AUTHOR

Edward W. Miller has an extensive knowledge and experience in meditative practices and non-dual Inquiry tools. This knowledge has been the foundational development of his transformative SoulTranSync practice. Over his 25-year spiritual journey, he has gained wisdom and invaluable training tools to help others realize innovative meditative skills that foster life changing results.

As a student of Transcendental and Buddhist Meditation practices, and progressive modalities of Self-Inquiry through NonDuality, he has researched and studied many great metaphysical teachers— including Eckhart Tolle, Mooji, Adyashanti, Chogyan Trungpa, Byron Katie and Ihaleakala Hew Len, Ph.D. But of all his study, he has been most impressed and personally transformed by the Hawaiian forgiveness teaching of Ho'oponopono.

Using these Best Practices, Edward has designed the SoulTranSync practices and tools, to inspire more peace, love, forgiveness and happiness through group workshops and individual coaching clients. His goal is always to direct you towards awakening your inner nature and genuine spirit in order to live a more fulfilling life. He also instills that suffering of any variety is completely optional and avoidable if living in the NOW or present moment.

For upcoming events, resources, and information on how to work with Edward, visit his website:

www.SoulTranSync.com